Early Utilitarians

Ken Binmore

Early Utilitarians

Lives and Ideals

 Springer

Ken Binmore
London, UK

ISBN 978-3-030-74582-0   ISBN 978-3-030-74583-7 (eBook)
https://doi.org/10.1007/978-3-030-74583-7

© The Editor(s) (if applicable) and The Author(s), under exclusive license to Springer Nature Switzerland AG 2021

This work is subject to copyright. All rights are solely and exclusively licensed by the Publisher, whether the whole or part of the material is concerned, specifically the rights of translation, reprinting, reuse of illustrations, recitation, broadcasting, reproduction on microfilms or in any other physical way, and transmission or information storage and retrieval, electronic adaptation, computer software, or by similar or dissimilar methodology now known or hereafter developed.

The use of general descriptive names, registered names, trademarks, service marks, etc. in this publication does not imply, even in the absence of a specific statement, that such names are exempt from the relevant protective laws and regulations and therefore free for general use.

The publisher, the authors and the editors are safe to assume that the advice and information in this book are believed to be true and accurate at the date of publication. Neither the publisher nor the authors or the editors give a warranty, expressed or implied, with respect to the material contained herein or for any errors or omissions that may have been made. The publisher remains neutral with regard to jurisdictional claims in published maps and institutional affiliations.

This Springer imprint is published by the registered company Springer Nature Switzerland AG
The registered company address is: Gewerbestrasse 11, 6330 Cham, Switzerland

This book is dedicated to

Brian Skyrms

a good friend and a wise counsellor

Contents

1	**Introduction**	**1**
2	**Shaftesbury**	**3**
	2.1 Where to Start?	3
	2.2 Lord Shaftesbury	4
	2.3 Shaftesbury's Life and Times	6
	2.4 Leveling Down?	7
	2.5 Was Shaftesbury a Utilitarian?	7
3	**Hutcheson**	**9**
	3.1 The First Utilitarian	9
	3.2 The Scottish Enlightenment	9
	3.3 Hutcheson's Life and Times	10
	3.4 The Moral Sense	11
	3.5 Utopia?	15
4	**Helvétius**	**17**
	4.1 De L'Esprit	17
	4.2 Les Philosophes	17
	4.3 Personal Morality or Public Policy?	19
	4.4 Act or Rule Utilitarianism?	20
	4.5 Helvétius's Life	20
5	**Hume**	**23**
	5.1 Hume's Life	23
	5.2 Utility	24
	5.3 Sympathy and Empathy	26
	5.4 Convention	26
6	**Beccaria**	**29**
	6.1 Crime and Punishment	29
	6.2 Still Worth Reading	29
	6.3 Enforcement	30
	6.4 Beccaria's Life and Times	30

7 Godwin — 33
- 7.1 Physician, Heal Thyself! — 33
- 7.2 Political Justice — 33
- 7.3 Godwin's Life — 34

8 Bentham — 39
- 8.1 Bentham and Mill? — 39
- 8.2 Termites and Moths — 39
- 8.3 Bentham's Foundations — 41
- 8.4 Bentham's Life — 44
- 8.5 Bentham's Unfinished Agenda — 45

9 Mill — 47
- 9.1 Successor to Bentham — 47
- 9.2 Utilitarianism and Liberty — 48
- 9.3 Mill's Obituary of Bentham — 49

10 Jevons — 51
- 10.1 Cardinal Utility? — 51
- 10.2 Jevon's Life — 53
- 10.3 Summary — 54

11 Sidgwick — 55
- 11.1 Termite or Moth? — 55
- 11.2 What Kind of Hedonism? — 56
- 11.3 Sidgwick's Life and Times — 57

12 Edgeworth — 59
- 12.1 Irish Polymath — 59
- 12.2 Fair Taxation — 60
- 12.3 Edgeworth's Life — 61

13 Hare — 63
- 13.1 Utilitarianism in Retreat — 63
- 13.2 Preference Utilitarianism — 64
- 13.3 Prescriptivity — 64
- 13.4 Universalizability — 66
- 13.5 Hare's Life — 67

14 Rawls — 69
- 14.1 Rawls a Utilitarian? — 69
- 14.2 Reflective Equilibrium — 70
- 14.3 Original Position — 71
- 14.4 Why Maximin? — 73
- 14.5 Deducing Utilitarianism — 74
- 14.6 Bentham's Unfinished Agenda — 75
- 14.7 Gentleman and Scholar — 76

14.8 Naturalizing Rawls 76

15 Harsanyi 79
15.1 Crying in the Wilderness? 79
15.2 Neoclassical Cardinal Utility 81
15.3 Two Defenses of Utilitarianism 83
15.4 Interpersonal Comparison 85
15.5 Harsanyi Doctrine? 86
15.6 Harsanyi's Life 88
15.7 Bentham's Unfinished Agenda 89

Further Reading   91

Index   93

Chapter 1

Introduction

Why look back over the lives and ideals of utilitarian pioneers? I have three reasons. The first is to ask why the culture of their times leads philosophers to neglect certain issues in favor of others. Why, for example, was the naturalism of ancient Greeks like Democritus and Epicurus left on a back burner for two thousand years until reinvented by enlightenment thinkers, of whom Hutcheson and Hume are examples in this book? Why are the various proponents of modern psychological approaches to studying happiness reinventing the wheels already invented by such early utilitarians? Why are modern philosophers equally reluctant to learn that modern economists no longer identify utility with happiness? Could it be that those who neglect history are compelled to repeat it?

The second reason is to trace the thoughts on utilitarianism offered in my own book *Natural Justice* back to their origins. The book is an evolutionary reinterpretation of the work of the modern philosophers John Rawls and John Harsanyi that is heavily dependent on the naturalism of the great David Hume. Where did they get their ideas from? On whose shoulders did they stand?

The third reason is to attempt to try once more to gain some recognition in the philosophy profession for John Harsanyi's success in providing answers to the questions that Jeremy Bentham—generally acknowledged as the founding father of modern utilitarianism—raised but left unanswered. For this reason, my definition of early utilitarian work extends all the way to the 1950s, when the debate between Rawls and Harsanyi was in full swing.

I am by no means the first person to attempt a history of utilitarian thought, but I think I am the first person to attempt an account in which the things that really matter are not buried under layers of scholarly commentary or mathematical abstraction. There are no equations in this short book, and very few references, which seem to me superfluous now that we can google anything we want to look up. I apologize to those who would have preferred a more traditional book. On the other hand, much of the problem that utilitarianism faced in getting established was too much respect for the traditions of the past.

Chapter 2
Shaftesbury

2.1 Where to Start?

Praising those who put the public good before their own personal interests doubtless goes back into prehistoric times, but the public good in such commendations is never defined in the precise way that modern utilitarians think essential. A lecture that Plato gave at the Academy he founded in ancient Athens is perhaps the best exemplar of the ancient attitude. The lecture apparently caused consternation among the students for its claim that the Good is to be found among the abstract ideals of which Plato thought the world of our senses is a mere shadow, but it eventually became the philosophical basis of early Christian theology.

Should one therefore regard Plato as a utilitarian? Philosophers say *no*, because Plato's notion of an absolute Good is too distant from the utilitarian ideal. Rationalist philosophers like Plato think you can determine the nature of the Good by divorcing yourself from ordinary life, and applying Reason to the problem. But different rationalists turned out to have different thoughts about what Reason entails. Only in modern times has any kind of consensus emerged that derives a utilitarian structure for the Good from a set of arguably self-evident axioms.[1]

What of the less grandiose ideas of Aristotle? Rather than some ideal metaphysical Good, he sees no need to look beyond the down-to-earth notion of happiness, so anticipating Jeremy Bentham by more than two thousand years. He tells us his thoughts on how happiness is to be achieved, but they apply only to well-off folk like himself, living a comfortable life in a small Greek city, so Bentham's dictum that everybody should count for one—and nobody for more than one—had no place in his system.

A few years later, the philosopher Epicurus was also teaching that what matters is seeking pleasure and avoiding pain, but he included women and slaves in his small community in ancient Athens. John Stuart Mill was therefore willing to count Epicurus as a utilitarian, but Epicurus thought it necessary to withdraw from city life rather than seeking to promote the sum of happiness in society as a whole.

---
[1] The axioms and derivation in John Broome's *Weighing Goods* are particularly elegant.

Epicurus is perhaps the nearest philosophers got to modern utilitarianism until the time of the Enlightenment, where this chapter begins. The Stoics, for example, substituted virtue for happiness.[2] Later philosophers drifted back to the ideals of Plato. The neoplatonism of Plotinus, for example, became the philosophical backdrop to early Christian thought. St Thomas Aquinas risked accusations of heresy in replacing Plato by Aristotle in the thirteenth century. However, only Aristotle's logical and metaphysical work was thought worthy of inclusion in Aquinas's attempt to create a natural theology, in which the existence of God was to to be a conclusion rather than an assumption. Such accusations of heresy were a major obstacle not only to natural theology, but also to the later development of utilitarian ideas in the centuries that followed.

Utilitarian ideas kept surfacing every now and again over the years, but it was not until the seventeenth century that the intellectual climate was ready for utilitarianism as we understand it today. It would have been possible to start with John Gay and other Christian writers who experimented with utilitarian ideas not long before Shaftesbury, with whom I have chosen to begin. He came nowhere near getting his teeth into the foundational issues that motivate this book, but the scene needs to be set if we are to understand why utilitarianism was so long in gestation.

2.2 Lord Shaftesbury

Anthony Ashley-Cooper was the third Earl of Shaftesbury. He is sometimes confused with the seventh Earl, who was a famous Victorian reformer and philanthropist. He can also be confused with his grandfather, the first Earl of Shaftesbury, who was a big wheel in the politics of his day, but mostly remembered today as the patron of the philosopher John Locke.

In the next chapter, we shall hear more of Locke's role in providing philosophical justifications for the Glorious Revolution of 1688 that put an end to the turbulent era surrounding the English Civil War, in which the first Earl was one of many shuttlecocks battered by both cavaliers and roundheads for his attempts at finding compromises. However, the first Earl is relevant here only for establishing the liberal traditions of his family, and for bringing up his grandson after his parents fell out with each other. Our Lord Shaftesbury therefore had the good fortune to be tutored by John Locke, although he went his own distinctive way when he started to write philosophy himself.

Utilitarian pioneer? Shaftesbury is regarded as a utilitarian pioneer for the kind of reforming zeal that led him to write:

> To love the Publick, to study universal Good, and to promote the Interest of the whole World, as far as lies within our power, is surely the Height of Goodness.

Such quotes make Shaftesbury typical of a benevolent theme that runs through the whole of philosophical history, but he makes no attempt to quantify his moral

---

[2] Stoicism was founded by Zeno of Citium, who lived in Athens at the same time as Epicurus.

2.2. LORD SHAFTESBURY

intuitions. There is certainly no hint of the idea that the sum of some correlate of utility should be maximized. However, his influence on Francis Hutcheson is very strong—so strong that we can delay discussion of the precise form his contributions to the foundations of utilitarianism took until the next chapter. Shaftesbury himself was decidedly hostile to any kind of metaphysical system-building, which perhaps explains a number of apparent inconsistencies in his own writings that have led to a good deal of critical dispute on precisely where he stood on various issues. Hutcheson, on the other hand, offers tidy versions of both Shaftesbury's naturalism and his utopianism, shorn of irrelevant distractions.

My own view is that Shaftesbury is most interesting as illustrating the transition from the doctrinaire prejudices of the dark ages to the more scientific attitudes of the age of the enlightenment. He was, in particular, an important pioneer in promoting an empirical approach to moral questions. We are not to imagine that pure Reason is adequate to allow us to deduce what morality should prescribe. We must look instead to the moral sentiments we find within ourselves if we are to understand why morality matters to the human race.

The internal moral sense to which he appeals is admittedly planted in us by a wholly benevolent God, but even the existence of God is defended by an appeal to the Argument by Design, in which the empirical evidence for design seemed incontrovertible before the evolutionary ideas we nowadays take for granted had been conceived. This venture into naturalism was influential among the Parisian philosophes of the next age, discussed briefly in the chapter on Helvétius. Both Diderot and Voltaire mention Shaftesbury with approval.

Benevolence? Shaftesbury's naturalism is tempered by his utopian instincts. We are not to follow Machiavelli or Hobbes in attributing all human motivation to nothing more than self-love. The evidence that we are social animals says otherwise.[3] But he went totally overboard on the idea that our selfish urges can somehow be subordinated to the instinct for benevolence that God has built into human nature. This utopianism continues to plague utilitarianism to this day, but was especially strong among Victorian utilitarians like William Godwin.

Shaftesbury was impatient with the model of human behavior as pure selfishness promoted by Hobbes in his notorious *Leviathan*, in which he argues that it is rational for us to surrender our autonomy to an absolute sovereign rather than live in the state of nature to which we would otherwise be condemned, which Hobbes famously characterizes as being "solitary, poor, nasty, brutish, and short". Shaftesbury anticipates Hume in denying that such social contract models are viable.[4] It is typical of Shaftesbury's style that he should point out that Hobbes' model of human nature as pure selfishness does not even apply to Hobbes himself—otherwise Hobbes would not have written *Leviathan* with a view to improving the way our societies work.

---

[3] The idea that reciprocity can explain how self-love can be reconciled with cooperative behavior had to wait for David Hume—although it was not until modern times that his idea gained any traction through the support it finds in the theory of games.

[4] Because there is no reason why we should feel obliged to honor the hypothetical promises made by our mythical ancestors when they supposedly surrendered their autonomy for the security to be found in an authoritarian state.

2.3 Shaftesbury's Life and Times

Shaftesbury (1671–1713) was made a ward of his grandfather at the age of three after his parents fell out very badly. His mother apparently threatened to refuse to see him unless he cut off relations with his father. John Locke found him an apt pupil, and they remained good friends in later life, but Shaftesbury differed quite sharply from his tutor on a number of philosophical issues. However, he remained true to the family tradition established by his grandfather in supporting the Whig ascendency that eventually followed the English Civil War.

Glorious Revolution. This perhaps the place to say something about the aftermath of the English Civil War, without some knowledge of which it is impossible to understand the origins of utilitarianism. Shaftesbury's grandfather fought first as a cavalier—in support of the King—and then as a roundhead—in support of Parliament, which eventually won the war. But the attempt to rule the country as a democratic republic foundered, and the experiment ended with Oliver Cromwell operating a military dictatorship.

After the chaos that followed Cromwell's death, Shaftesbury's grandfather supported the restoration of the son of the executed Charles I to the English throne as King Charles II, but the Catholic beliefs and authoritarian attitudes of his brother James II when he succeeded to the throne led his grandfather to switch sides yet again in favor of replacing James by his Protestant daughter Mary, and her constitutionally minded husband, William of Orange, whose 1688 invasion of England from the Netherlands was largely unopposed.

However, the Tory opposition to the Whiggish innovations that followed the Glorious Revolution of 1688 remained strong. The first earl was dead by this time, but life became difficult again for the prominent Shaftesbury family when Mary's sister Anne succeeded to the throne, and formed a Tory administration. Indeed, the Whig ascendancy remained at risk until the 1745 uprising led by Bonnie Prince Charlie—the son of James II—was finally crushed at the Battle of Culloden.

Youth. After the death of his grandfather in 1683, Shaftesbury was sent to a Tory school where his Whiggish beliefs were unappreciated. But at the age of fifteen he was allowed his freedom, which he used to embark on a grand tour of Europe with some older companions. He returned to England in !689, the year after the Glorious Revolution, in which the authoritarian James II was expelled from England in favor of William and Mary, who undertook to rule constitutionally. He eventually succeeded his father as the third Earl, after which he sat as a Whig in the House of Lords. Before then, he was elected to the House of Commons, but ill health forced him to retire in 1698.

Works. The works that made Shaftesbury famous were mostly written in the period 1701–1710. His utilitarian sentiments are to be found in his *Inquiry concerning Virtue or Merit*, a revised version of which is included in the three-volume *Characteristicks of Men, Manners, Opinions, Times*, a final edition of which appeared a year after his death in 1714.

The *Characteristicks* also includes his views on such subjects as why jokes are funny, and why beautiful things are pleasing. It is typical of Shaftesbury that he does not separate such topics from his approach to morality. The debt that Francis Hutcheson owes to Shaftesbury is evident in the fact that Hutcheson also thinks the psychology of humor and aesthetics are relevant to understanding our moral sense, although this issue is downplayed in the chapter on Hutcheson coming next.

2.4 Leveling Down?

Shaftesbury's concern for the "universal good" was understood by later utilitarians as a demand for prioritizing the sum of human happiness. But whose happiness is to count? Jeremy Bentham expressed the later utilitarian attitude to this question by requiring that "everybody to count for one, and nobody for more than one".

Such egalitarian sentiments were commonplace in the aftermath of the English Civil War, as the roundhead proles found that they had risked all, but were still expected to continue in servitude to the propertied classes. The very name of a movement called the Levelers indicates the priorities of its membership. The times were therefore ready for reform, but it was not until Cesare Beccaria's *Crimes and Punishments* that the dam of reaction was finally breached. Without its widespread success among European intellectuals, perhaps Bentham's dictum would have fallen on stony ground.

2.5 Was Shaftesbury a Utilitarian?

Everybody agrees that Shaftesbury was a utilitarian pioneer, but is he to be counted as a real utilitarian?

This question exposes a philosophical ambiguity about who should be regarded as a utilitarian. Is a utilitarian somebody who thinks that people respond to the utility—or usefulness—of the goods and services that they encounter in their daily lives, rather than a do-gooder who thinks they know better what is good for people than they know themselves? Or does a utilitarian need to be someone who promotes the sum of everybody's utility? The first definition would imply that nearly all economists should be counted as utilitarians—even the libertarian fringe who think that markets are the solution to all social problems. But this book works with the second definition.

Of course, many authors who would not count as utilitarians according to the second definition would count as utilitarians according to the first definition. David Hume certainly satisfies the first definition, but does he satisfy the second definition? I think the answer is *no* because it is not enough that somebody should express sympathy with the idea that the public good should be promoted. It is necessary for the second definition to apply that an author offer some account of how the utilities of individual citizens are to be understood in order that it make sense to aggregate these utilities when passing judgement on a society. For this reason, I follow the literature in regarding Shaftesbury as a pre-utilitarian. Our first true utilitarian will be Francis Hutcheson in the next chapter, although many scholars would reserve their accolades for Jeremy Bentham in Chapter 8.

Chapter 3
Hutcheson

3.1 The First Utilitarian

One can identify the utilitarian ideal gradually taking form in a number of early writers like Shaftesbury, but I have chosen to regard Francis Hutcheson as the first true utilitarian. He certainly anticipated Jeremy Bentham by writing of the "greatest happiness for the greatest number" as early as 1728, when the Scottish Enlightenment was just getting off the ground.

The word *utility* was then new, having been adopted by pioneer economists of the period to register their belief that what people want are not philosophical abstractions, but things that are useful in their daily lives. Hutcheson captures this attitude by following Shaftesbury in treating morality as a natural phenomenon. The question of what should be regarded as a public good then becomes an empirical issue that he asks us to decide by looking within ourselves to examine our own moral intuitions. One does not have to follow where he wants to take this approach to recognize that it marks the beginning of the modern understanding of utilitarianism. Indeed, all the fundamental issues that still trouble utilitarians had already been raised by Hutcheson, and his French contemporary Helvétius (whose thoughts are the focus of the next chapter).

3.2 The Scottish Enlightenment

The period of enlightenment that finally put an end to the dark ages is usually held to be a phenomenon of the "long eighteenth century" (1685–1815). It reached its zenith in 1751 with the publication in Paris of the first volume of the Encyclopédie that eventually ran to many volumes, with articles written by hundreds of intellectuals who called themselves "les philosophes". It enjoyed a late flourishing in Scotland for which the work of Hutcheson serves here as a taking-off point. He was not such a great philosopher as his successor David Hume—whose philosophy bears comparison with the greatest ever written. Nor was he to produce anything nearly as influential as Adam Smith's *Wealth of Nations*. But Francis Hutcheson came first.

The philosophers of the Scottish enlightenment were above all naturalists in their approach to understanding the world. Their attitude is summarized by the title of Thomas Reid's book *Common Sense*. They were going to do their own thinking for themselves without depending on the authority of the past, no matter how distinguished its proponents might have been. Insofar as they were influenced by previous thinkers, John Locke was their hero.

Locke not only endorsed the thoughts of the ancient empiricists, but had become the prophet of the liberalized regime in Great Britain that followed the Glorious Revolution of 1688. At the same time, he was no dangerous radical. His blank-slate empiricism explicitly excluded mathematics, morality and religion. The removal of religion from the arena of debate was particularly important in the Scotland of the time, since nobody wanted to share the fate of Thomas Aikenhead, hanged in Edinburgh at the age of twenty for the crime of blasphemy as recently as 1697 for a few thoughtless words. Not that Francis Hutcheson would have had any wish to blaspheme. His Presbyterian faith was sufficiently strong that it even led to his adding his voice to those who spoke against any academic recognition of David Hume on account of his suspected atheism.

It is perhaps useful to take Locke as an example of the need to put oneself in the shoes of thinkers of their own time when evaluating intellectual pioneers, rather than looking down upon them from the shoulders of the giants who followed up their ideas. There was no understanding of genetics when Locke argued that the mind is a *tabula rasa* on which experience can write anything whatever. There was no systematic anthropological data to guide his attempt to trace our current social contract from its putative origins among savage ancestors like the recently discovered natives of North America. In a world in which David Hume observes in passing that species are immutable, the theory of evolution was inconceivable. With our current knowledge, Locke's Natural Laws seem contrived inventions designed to generate the conclusions that he favored, but he deserves our respect for contemplating laws that he genuinely regarded as natural in place of the metaphysical fancies of his philosophical predecessors.

The notion of an inbuilt moral intuition championed by Francis Hutcheson deserves to be respected for the same reason. We may think we know better now how to model the evolutionary origins of our sense of morality, but Hutcheson was writing at a time when seeking to look within your own natural self for inspiration on what should count as good or right was to step forward out of the darkness that had gone before.

3.3 Hutcheson's Life and Times

Francis Hutcheson (1694–1746) was born into the colony of Scottish Protestants planted less than a hundred years before among the Gaelic-speaking Catholics of Northern Ireland. The unrest created by this attempt to make Ireland governable from London persists to this day.

Hutcheson succeeded his father and grandfather as a Presbyterian minister. After attending the University of Glasgow, he was invited to set up a nonconformist academy in Dublin. He chose to accept the invitation rather than to pursue a career as a Presbyterian minister himself. He found Dublin congenial, and eventually married a local girl. A son was born whom he named after himself.

Hutcheson's important works were published anonymously in Dublin during this period. He shows the debt he owes to Shaftesbury in treating our regard for virtue as akin to our liking for beautiful things. However, his 1725 contribution to aesthetics called *An Inquiry into the Original of Our Ideas of Beauty and Virtue* is sufficiently original that it remains of interest to this day. It develops Locke's psychological distinction between primary and secondary qualities in a manner that modern scholarship still values. However, we focus on his 1728 *Essay on the Nature and Conduct of the Passions and Affections, with Illustrations of the Moral Sense*. On the strength of this work, Hutcheson was appointed to the Chair of Moral Philosophy at the University of Glasgow in the following year. Adam Smith succeeded to the same chair in 1752.

Hutcheson did not add to his output in any serious way after his move to Glasgow. He devoted himself instead to the university, which he felt needed a good deal of modernizing. One innovation was his lecturing in English rather than Latin like his predecessors. The lively style inherited from the Dublin preaching tradition, also helped to make him a popular lecturer. As was not uncommon in those days, his liberal attitudes got him into trouble on more than one occasion with the Presbyterian Church. In 1738, he was accused of heresy for arguing that it is possible for people to have a knowledge of good and evil without any knowledge of God.[1] But he survived largely unscathed until his death in 1745.

A year after his death, his son and namesake published another edition of his *Illustrations on the Moral Sense*. In 1755, he published and edited a version of his father's *A System of Moral Philosophy*, written for college students.[2]

Hutcheson's reputation as father of the Scottish Enlightenment remains unchallenged. Thomas Reid cited him in his writings. David Hume sought his opinion on a preliminary version of the section "Of Human Morals" in his *Treatise of Human Nature*. Adam Smith sat in his lectures as a student. Even Immanuel Kant, who was very proud of his Scottish grandfather, was influenced by him.

3.4 The Moral Sense

In Hutcheson's view, human beings have a variety of internal senses besides our five external senses, including a sense of beauty, of morality, of honor, and of the ridiculous. Of these, Hutcheson followed Shaftesbury in considering the moral

---

[1] Accusations of heresy were a serious occupational hazard in those days. Even today, nonconformist preachers are not entirely safe. An acquaintance of mine somehow contrived to get himself excommunicated for heresy by the Methodist Church only a few years ago.

[2] Hutcheson's work has been conveniently packaged by Robin Downie in his *Francis Hutcheson: Philosophical Writings*. Downie was a modern successor of Francis Hutcheson and Adam Smith in the Chair of Moral Philosophy at the University of Glasgow.

sense to be the most important. He believed that it is implanted in us by God, and pronounces "instinctively and immediately on the character of actions and affections, approving those that are virtuous and disapproving those that are vicious".

Hutcheson's moral criterion was whether or not an act tends to promote the general welfare of mankind. In doing so, he anticipated the utilitarianism of the English thinker Jeremy Bentham, even to his use of the famous phrase:

The greatest happiness for the greatest number,

which is almost universally attributed to Bentham.

Greatest happiness? One can only maximize one quantity at a time, and so to speak of the greatest happiness for the greatest number is ambiguous. So it is not clear why being the first to have mouthed the phrase has been so hotly disputed.[3] The ambiguity is evident in Derek Parfit's modern attempt to ridicule the utilitarian ethos. His "repugnant conclusion" observes that the individual utilities of the citizens in a society may be repugnantly small, but one can still make the sum of their utilities as large as one likes by expanding the population size to some enormous value.

One can respond that there would be no point in proposing reforms at all if the shape a society takes leaves the utility of its citizens unaltered, but in accepting Hutcheson's ambiguous phrase as an informal definition of utilitarianism, it seems safer to interpret it as meaning "the greatest happiness for the whole population" without attempting to pretend that it offers a solution to problems that Hutcheson did not envisage.[4]

Naturalism? From the point of view of a scholar seeking to understand the constraints that their contemporary intellectual environment imposes on thinkers, it is striking that Hutcheson should spend so many pages defending his view that the moral sense should be studied from a naturalistic perspective. Nowadays such an approach would be taken to imply that Hutcheson plans to attempt an evolutionary explanation of the origins of human morality, but the theory of evolution was unknown in his time. Most philosophers who thought of themselves as scientific called themselves Deists. They attributed our existence to an original act of creation by a Deity who afterwards left the world to run under its own steam. But Hutcheson was firm in his Presbyterian beliefs. When he called for a naturalistic approach, he merely meant that we should look within ourselves to examine our own moral sense in seeking to determine its properties.

His negative attitude to the following list of approaches to morality current in his time therefore needs to be evaluated from Hutcheson's perceived need to defend a version of naturalism that had been out of favor since the time of such ancient philosophers as Democritus and Epicurus.

---

[3] For example, R. Shackleton "The greatest happiness of the greatest number: The history of Bentham's phrase". *Studies on Voltaire and the Eighteenth Century*, 90 (1972), 1461-1482.

[4] Unlike John Stuart Mill, who is taken to task by Francis Edgeworth for fudging the ambiguity in the original phrase.

3.4. THE MORAL SENSE

Sympathy? To approve of virtue in other people and to disapprove of vice is to express a preference. Hutcheson is very concerned that such a moral preference should not be confused with a person's personal or selfish preferences. As he points out, moral preferences cannot be classified under the same heading as preferences for such things as more money or better food because we do not commend or condemn someone for wanting to eat well or seek advancement for their children as we do for their activities on behalf of the general welfare of a society.

The pleasure that some people feel at making others happy is therefore treated as just one more example of a personal preference. So he anticipates modern economists in regarding what they sometimes call sympathetic preferences—which recognize a person's concern for the welfare of others—as no different in kind from their selfish concerns with their own individual welfare. Such sympathetic preferences stem from our self-love, and are to be carefully distinguished from the benevolence that derives from the instinctive application of our moral sense.

Hutcheson even anticipates Immanuel Kant's view that to do something for others because you take pleasure in doing so should not be counted as moral at all. He accepts that people often have mixed motives, but to the extent that you help or hinder others, you deserve more or less approval depending on the extent to which your motives are unselfish. St Francis of Assisi is famous for taking joy in helping others, but Hutcheson would perhaps have argued that this famous exemplar of selflessness was not acting morally at all.

There are authors who argue that the great David Hume learned everything he knew from Hutcheson, but denying the relevance of sympathetic preferences to morality is only one of many issues on which they parted company. As Hume comments:

> What theory of morals can ever serve any useful purpose, unless it can show ... that all the duties it recommends are also the true interest of each individual?

Sometimes this quote is mischievously interpreted to mean that Hume believes that no theory of morals can serve any useful purpose whatever, so it may be helpful to use the example of the rationality of voting to clarify his meaning.

It is commonly said that it is irrational to vote in a national election because there is a cost to voting in time and trouble, but the probability that a single vote will affect the outcome is negligible. Hutcheson would presumably have replied that our moral sense tells us that we should vote anyway because we ought to put the public welfare ahead of our own private concerns. Hume would have responded that such an argument cannot evade the necessity of comparing the strength of our moral preferences with our personal preferences. How much do we need to value the welfare of society as a whole to outweigh our own individual welfare?[5]

More generally, Hutcheson leaves open a question that is to plague utilitarianism to this day. If utilitarianism is to be treated as a system of personal morality, why should anyone follow its precepts rather than their own personal preferences?

---

[5] The political scientist Andrew Gelman recently did some accountancy for the voting problem in US presidential elections. He estimated the probability of a single vote being pivotal in some states at one in ten million, but federal expenditure is of the order of twelve trillion dollars. But how does one compare a dollar you spend on yourself with a dollar spent by Washington?

The answer offered by most modern philosophers is to propose that morality lives in a separate domain from our day-to-day lives. For example, John Rawls—commonly said to be the greatest moral philosopher of the last century—tells us that we have a Natural Duty to honor his egalitarian conception of justice as fairness. John Harsanyi extracts a utilitarian rabbit from the same hat, but he too relies on something called Moral Commitment to evade the issue of why we should put the sum of all utilities ahead of our own utility.

My own theory attempts the apparently impossible task of reconciling these Kantian approaches with the naturalism of Hutcheson and Hume, in which such inventions as Natural Duty or Moral Commitment are necessarily rejected as what Daniel Dennett calls skyhooks. However, the circle is squared only at the expense of abandoning the notion of utilitarianism as a system of personal morality in favor of the idea of Helvétius that it should rather be seen as an instrument for the guidance of a benign government seeking the approval of the citizens it governs.

Reason? There is a long-standing division among philosophers between rationalists and empiricists. Layfolk are surprised to find that this division does not imply that empiricists are thought to be irrational. Philosophical rationalists are simply philosophers who feel able to decide contingent propositions about the world without the need for any evidence. Immanuel Kant, for example, thought that no evidence was necessary to determine that space is Euclidean.

Kant is even more famous for his claim that rationality requires obeying his categorical imperative that tells us "to act on the maxim through which you can at the same time will that it be a universal law". This imperative is said to be categorical because it is to be obeyed whatever the circumstances. Kant tells us that it implies in particular that we must never lie—not even to a murderous axeman asking where your neighbor is to be found. Rules like this that take no account of the consequences of an action are said to be deontological in contrast to the overt consequentialism of a utilitarian like Hutcheson.

Hutcheson's insistence that we must look within ourselves to determine the nature of our moral sense makes him an empiricist. As with much else, his denial that Reason alone is adequate for this purpose is taken to its logical extreme by David Hume:

> If we take in our hand any volume; of divinity or school metaphysics, for instance; let us ask, Does it contain any abstract reasoning concerning quantity or number? No. Does it contain any experimental reasoning concerning matter of fact and existence? No. Commit it then to the flames: for it can contain nothing but sophistry and illusion.

Hutcheson's consequentialist views are similarly given lively expression when David Hume tells us that Reason is the slave of the passions. As he put it: "It is not contrary to reason to prefer the destruction of the whole world to the scratching of my finger."

Convention. Hutcheson ties himself up in knots over the word fitness, which now seems to have even more meanings than in his time. Nowadays, a naturalist speaking of fitness would mean the kind of biological fitness that evolution tends to maximize. A health enthusiast would mean the kind of fitness of the body sought by those naturalists who delight in exposing their naked bodies to the sun. An agony aunt might agree that Alice's T-shirt fits her body snugly, but advise that it is not fitting that she wear it to a black-tie event. This last sense best captures the kind of fitness that Hutcheson thinks matters. How fitting is it that we should honor our moral sense? To what extent does it accord with the moral sense of others?

However, he would not go nearly as far as Hume in treating our sense of morality as a matter of convention. The moral relativism implicit in such an identification would probably have struck him as utterly unacceptable. On the other hand, his notion that we can identify what counts as moral by exploring those unselfish actions of which we approve or disapprove fits the idea that our moral sense is conventional like a glove.

To survive, a convention needs to be what game theorists call a Nash equilibrium of a society's game of life. That is to say, each player must be optimizing given the behavior of the other players. Those who follow a convention's precepts therefore need to be rewarded with approval or better, and those who deviate need to be punished with disapproval or worse. However, it would be getting ahead of ourselves to say any more at this point, since part of Hume's chapter is devoted to his largely original views on how conventions work.

3.5 Utopia?

Hutcheson does not regard himself as part of the social contract literature that begins with Grotius and Pufendorf, and continues through Hobbes, Locke, Rousseau, and Kant. The idea is that human beings once lived in a state of nature from which our current civilization developed as we learned to cooperate with one another.

Grotius and Pufendorf had the idea that a concourse of ancient sages got together, and agreed a contract that specifies the rules that govern our cooperative behavior till this day. David Hume would have nothing to do with this notion of an original contract, even if extended to admit a series of smaller meetings of sages. He pointed out that even if such constitutional meetings ever took place, their agreements would not be contractual without a legal system to enforce their provisions. Our ancestors may have made promises on our behalf, but surely we are not bound to keep even a promise of our own for no better reason than that we have promised to honor it?

Hutcheson sees no need to concern himself with such questions of enforcement. For him, it was enough that our moral sense calls for us all to join in securing the greatest happiness for the greatest number. He followed Shaftesbury in reacting badly to any suggestion that we are not primarily benevolent creatures. He was particularly displeased with Bernard Mandeville's satirical poem *The Fable of the Bees*, which describes a bee community thriving until their economy collapses as a consequence of the bees becoming honest and virtuous. This idea that there can be no public benefit without private vices was anathema to Hutcheson.

Hutcheson was nearly as displeased with Thomas Hobbes' notion of a social contract, in which we supposedly trade a precarious existence in a state of nature that is famously "solitary, poor, nasty, brutish, and short" for the safety to be found in living under an absolute sovereign.

Hutcheson preferred the Lockean social contract story, in which our natural rights include the requirement that "No one ought to harm another in his life, health, liberty, or possessions". Property rights can then only be transferred in a civilized way. They are supposedly originally acquired by mixing one's labor with property in a state of nature that precedes ownership, provided "enough and as good is left in common for others". Hutcheson writes at length in a similar vein itemizing a plethora of supposedly natural laws and duties that govern the conduct of a moral society.

Hutcheson was therefore firmly in the utopian tradition that includes Shaftesbury, Locke and Rousseau. Jean-Jacques Rousseau's notion that the human species was born free as noble savages, but is now everywhere in chains remains popular to this day. The tradition flourished particularly strongly in the nineteenth century with the attempts of utopian socialists like Robert Owen and Josiah Wedgewood to found ideal communities that sometimes persisted for years at a time. Karl Marx was particularly hostile to this kind of impractical utopianism on the grounds that it merely served to hinder the efforts of revolutionary realists like himself.

The chapter on the philosopher William Godwin is a kind of rake's progress of a utopian dreamer. He tried determinedly over his whole life to uphold the principle that we should all live on the assumption that everybody will put the good of the community before their own selfish concerns, but he found that few people were as generous as Wedgewood when the public good demanded that Godwin receive yet another subsidy to fund his campaign for utopian reform.

How come such utopian aspirations won the hearts of so many intelligent folk in the nineteenth century? Could it be that the determinedly irrational Romantic reaction to the Enlightenment—fired particularly by Rousseau—was a parallel phenomenon? To what extent are we now gripped in a similar outbreak of impractical idealism? Where are the hard heads like Adam Smith and David Hume to set us straight? No-platformed perhaps, as Hutcheson sought to no-platform Hume in denying him support for a Chair in Edinburgh.

Chapter 4
Helvétius

4.1 De L'Esprit

Hutcheson would not have approved of Claude Adrien Helvétius (1715–1771) one little bit. Nor did the Catholic Church or King Louis XV of France, who had all traceable copies of his 1758 book *De l'Esprit* burned in the street by the Parisian hangman.[1] Helvétius had presumably been counting on the tolerance hitherto shown to les philosophes of the Encyclopédie, and the favor shown to him by the Queen, but when the full might of the state was turned against him, he wrote three humiliating retractions, after which he kept out of France for a while, first in England and then in Prussia, where he had an invitation from the philosophically minded Frederick the Great.

In retrospect, Louis XV's public condemnation of *De L'Esprit* could not have spread its materialistic doctrines more widely if he had tried. The scandal resulted in the book being hastily translated into many languages. It was certainly read, for example, by Jeremy Bentham—who gave Helvétius credit as the originator of utilitarianism—and by the influential Italian criminologist, Cesare Beccaria.

4.2 Les Philosophes

Who were the Parisian philosophers whose toleration led Helvétius to think he could get away with flouting the prejudices of an age gone by? A few anecdotes will have to suffice, since a whole book would not be adequate to document their efforts on behalf of the Enlightenment under the most reactionary government in Europe.

Les philosophes were seriously worried by the example made of Helvétius, which was clearly intended as a shot across their bows. It was possible to argue, for example, that Helvétius had borrowed all his ideas from Diderot—the prime mover in the project of the Encyclopédie—although this would be to ignore the reasons that

---
[1] *De l'Esprit* is usually translated as *On Mind* in contrast to Montesquieu's *De l'Esprit des Lois*, which is usually translated as *Spirit of the Laws*.

Helvétius is included here as a founder of the utilitarian movement. La Mettrie's book *L'Homme Machine,* arguing that human beings are merely soulless pieces of machinery, had taken materialism far beyond anything Helvétius proposed—although, like Voltaire, he had admittedly found it wiser to live abroad when things got too hot to remain in Paris. Les philosophes similarly thought it wise to suspend publication of the Encyclopédie for a while, until the fury of the establishment had blown itself out.

Diderot. The intellectual atmosphere of Paris in the middle of the eighteenth century was a curious mixture of respect for the reactionary government of Louis XV and the Catholic Church, and delight in some quarters for the new freedoms of the Enlightenment. Censorship was supposedly strict, but the censors themselves were often enlightened gentlemen. It was fashionable for aristocratic ladies to run intellectual salons in which radical opinions were freely debated with great enthusiasm.[2] Madame de Graffigny, for example, felt that everything fine in *De L'Esprit* had been had been learned in her own salon. Even the shy David Hume formed a relationship with the liberally minded Countess de Bouffler while in Paris, although it is hard to believe that she succeeded in taking his virginity.

Some philosophes, like the Baron d'Holbach, were aristocrats themselves, but making a reputation for yourself would have been more difficult for those of humble origin like Denis Diderot (1713–1784), or Jean-Jacques Rousseau (1712–1778).

Diderot was disowned by his father—who had doubtless scraped the financial barrel to fund his education—when he chose to become a writer instead of taking up a respectable profession. He himself scraped through a ramshackle life until rescued by Catherine the Great when all else had failed. It says something of Diderot's character, that Catherine complained that her interviews with him left her thighs black and blue where he had slapped them in his enthusiasm.

Like the other philosophes, Diderot wrote novels and plays as well as philosophy. Some were titillating, although only mildly pornographic by modern standards. His chief efforts over many years were devoted to organizing an encyclopedia of all the arts and sciences, to feature contributions from a wide range of authors, although he finished up writing many thousands of entries himself. He worked in harness with the mathematician d'Alembert to begin with, but d'Alembert abandoned the project in 1759, doubtless discouraged by the persecution they experienced for producing a work firmly espousing Enlightenment values. Diderot was eventually discouraged himself when he found that his printer—fearful of prosecution by the censor—had taken it upon himself to omit dangerous passages. But the Encyclopédie is remembered today as a beacon prefiguring the French Revolution, while the tedious works of his persecutors are forgotten.

Rousseau. It is a tribute to Diderot's good nature that he got on well with Rousseau over many years until Rousseau fell out with him, as he had fallen out

---

[2]I particularly like the fact that a *coup d'escalier* is a crushing retort that would have won the argument you just lost, if only you had thought of it before walking down the stairs on the way out of one of these salons.

with all the other philosophes. He even fell out with the amiable Hume, who sought to look after him when Rousseau decided to move to England after being exiled from France. Hume should have listened to the Baron d'Holbach, who warned him that he was warming a viper to his bosom.

To my mind, Rousseau was no great philosopher. The arguments in his *Inequality of Man* and *Social Contract* do not bear close examination. From the utilitarian perspective, he is only relevant as the inventor of a new skyhook called the General Will.[3] But he told people what they wanted to hear at a time when they wanted to hear it. For this reason he is lauded as the intellectual hero of the French Revolution. But far from promoting enlightenment values, the success of his novel *The New Héloise* and his play *Pygmalion* are said to have provided the impetus for the irrational Romantic movement that brought the Enlightenment to an end.

4.3 Personal Morality or Public Policy?

The philosophy of Helvétius was everything it was condemned for: atheistic and materialist—harking back two thousand years to Democritus and Epicurus. People are selfish. We are motivated solely by the pursuit of pleasure, and the avoidance of pain. There is no absolute Good or Evil. Our notions of good and evil are relative to the society in which we live. So there can be no such thing as an innate Moral Intuition. Nor indeed is any part of our intelligence innate. We are all supposedly born equal, our minds a blank slate on which education can write what it will. No wonder Louis XV was persuaded to have his work burned!

Hutcheson would have compared these foundational assumptions with those of Thomas Hobbes, whom he detested. How could Helvétius extract a version of utilitarianism from such an unpromising set of assumptions, for he certainly did argue that wise government should promote the general good?

The answer is that his version of utilitarianism is not about personal morality at all. So the problem of why we should promote the general good at the expense of our own selfish interests disappears. It is no longer necessary to invent philosophical skyhooks like Moral Commitment, or Natural Duty, or the General Will to bridge this yawning gap. But how is utilitarianism to be interpreted if not as a system of personal morality? Helvétius's answer is that utilitarianism makes better sense as a program of legislative action for a benign government seeking public approval.

Enforcement. Two vital questions left hanging in the air by Hutcheson are thereby answered. The first addresses the problem of public enforcement. Why follow the provisions of a utilitarian program, and not your own? Because breaking the law leads to punishment. The second question addresses the same problem, but applied to the government itself. Why care about the general good? Because even a ruler without sympathy for those he rules will perceive that rulers who do not enjoy

---

[3]Not to be confused with the Will of All. Its precepts are known only to those blessed with sublime wisdom. To implement the General Will, all individual wills must be brought into conformity with it.

the approval of their citizens are liable to be overthrown. James Madison made this point in the aftermath of the American Revolution. An unjust government risks creating a focal point around which an opposition can coalesce. Rival leaders then appear who appeal to the sense of fairness of their prospective followers.

If Louis XV had read *De L'Esprit* instead of burning it, perhaps his grandson Louis XVI would not have perished on the guillotine. But if Louis XV had not been a tyrant, so confident of his power that he allowed les philosophes enough freedom for their enlightened views to become fashionable, *De L'Esprit* would never have been written.

4.4 Act or Rule Utilitarianism?

The naturalism of Epicurus and his mentor Democritus had been systematically misrepresented by the early Christian Church as a sinful celebration of gluttony and lust. Their reputation had been rescued some hundred years before by the early French philosopher of science, Pierre Gassendi, but there is little sign of his having been at all influential with Helvétius. On the other hand, Helvétius had clearly read the delightful essays of Michel de Montaigne. One sign of this influence is his use of historical anecdotes to make particular philosophical points.

One story is perhaps the first contribution to an ongoing debate between act utilitarianism and rule utilitarianism. The Muslim sage Zaid—usually nowadays spelled Zayid—was troubled by assassins operating at night when acting as governor of Basra. He therefore imposed a curfew, breaches of which were punishable by death. The measure was successful in stemming the assassinations, but at the expense of the occasional execution of the innocent.

Helvétius would perhaps have said that the kind of utilitarianism which demands that each act a person makes must be chosen to maximize the sum of all utilities may make good sense when utilitarianism is interpreted as a system of personal morality, but only rule utilitarianism makes any sense when utilitarianism is interpreted as an instrument of public policy. Nevertheless, prominent modern utilitarians like John Harsanyi continue to defend rule utilitarianism as a system of personal morality, whereas critics like John Rawls find it unacceptably unfair that utilitarianism sometimes demands that a minority should suffer that the majority may prosper.

Suppose, for example, that an eye could be surgically removed from a sighted person and implanted in a blind person? Should some two-eyed people then be chosen to give up an eye so that the blind can see? If chosen, would it be moral to acquiesce to losing an eye? This standard story may seem fantastic, but it is enacted on a daily basis in the case of kidneys. There are even saints who volunteer unasked to give up a kidney to some unknown stranger.

4.5 Helvétius's Life

Helvétius was not Swiss as his name suggests, but born in Paris. His family had moved from Switzerland to France some generations before. His father was a physician following in the family tradition. It is significant for Helvétius that his father became the personal physician of Queen Marie Leszczynska, wife of Louis XV. She arranged that Helvétius be appointed a farmer-general—who were much hated tax collectors, famous for lining their own pockets. He then led a life of luxury, retiring early to indulge his artistic and intellectual tastes, His wife ran a famous salon for many years, and Helvétius was apparently generous in keeping some of the less successful philosophes afloat.

The condemnation of *De L'Esprit*—engineered perhaps by the jealousy of the Dauphine that he should be so favored by his mother—seems to have come as a bolt from the blue. But things had died down by the time Helvétius returned from Berlin, where he was favorably received by Frederick the Great. It was then that he retired to his country estate in France, where he was free with his money in relieving the distress of the poor, and the development of agriculture and technology. Few philosophers have succeeded in living so comfortable a life.

Chapter 5
Hume

5.1 Hume's Life

We have already heard a good deal about David Hume (1711–1776) in the chapters on Hutcheson and Helvétius. He became something of an intellectual celebrity among les philosophes while working in Paris, but chose to live in his native Edinburgh in spite of having to tolerate a good deal of disapproval from his fellow Scots. One story tells how he fell into a deep ditch while returning home after drinking too much at a convivial evening. A woman offered to help, but left him to flounder when she realized that he was David Hume, notorious for his supposed atheism.

Youth. Hume was born the younger son of a decayed family of Scottish gentlefolk. So he had to make his own way in the world. He did so by living in penury while developing his philosophical ideas, which he thought would bring him wealth and fame when his magnificent *Treatise on Human Nature* was published. But the book famously fell "dead-born from the press". He attributed its lack of success to his own literary failings rather than the prejudice of his potential audience, and tried again later with *An Enquiry Concerning Human Understanding*, which was somewhat more successful. His *Essays* were even better received, since they are full of good sense without challenging any philosophical or theological orthodoxies. However, he rescued himself financially by writing a history of England which eventually proved very popular, although even on this apparently safe subject, he had to overcome the hostility from the Whig ascendancy that greeted his initial volume on the first two Stuart Kings. After all, only a Tory would be willing to "shed a tear" for the executed Charles I.[1] He wisely left his skeptical *Dialogues concerning Natural Religion* to be published until after his death.

---

[1] John Stuart Mill went so far as to accuse David Hume of being condemned to play a Tory tune because his skepticism supposedly made it impossible for him to place any reliance on reason as an instrument for planning reform.

Character. In spite of his early disappointments, Hume was the most civilized, companiable, and contented of men. Even on his deathbed, he retained his good humor, totally disarming Samuel Johnson's biographer, James Boswell, when he tactlessly quizzed him on how it felt to be at death's door without a belief in the afterlife. As Boswell reports, "Mr Hume's pleasantry was such that there was no solemnity in the scene, and death for the time did not seem so dismal." In a less ghoulish deathbed conversation, Hume told Adam Smith that he had been reading Lucian's *Dialogues of the Dead*, in which various notables offer reasons to Charon why they should not be ferried across the Styx. When his own time came, he proposed to say, "Have a little patience, good Charon, I have been endeavouring to open the eyes of the Public. If I live a few years longer, I may have the satisfaction of seeing the downfall of some of the more prevailing systems of superstition." But then, says Hume, Charon would lose all patience, "You loitering rogue, that will not happen these many hundred years. Do you fancy I will grant you a lease for so long a term? Get into the boat, you lazy, loitering rogue."[2]

5.2 Utility

Some philosophers classify Hume as a utilitarian. It is true that he is free in his use of the word utility, whereas Hutcheson speaks of utility only very sparingly.

Was David Hume a utilitarian? I think not, because public utility for him was simply a way of referring to the practical usefulness of a public policy. He never speaks of utility as something that could be quantified. The idea that one person's utility might be compared with another's in the manner necessary to compute a sum of utilities is absent altogether. However, it may well be that utilitarianism would be called something else if Hume had not adopted the word utility, and so the opportunity is taken here to say something about its evolution.

Bernoulli. Accounts of the origins of the word utility trace its origins to the Latin *utilitas*. Its first use in its modern sense is said to date from as early as the fourteenth century, but commentators all agree on the significance of its adoption by Daniel Bernoulli in discussing the St Petersburg Paradox.

The paradox was invented by the Swiss mathematician Nicolaus Bernoulli, although it was actually his brother Daniel who published the paradox in a St Petersburg journal in 1738. The paradox concerns a casino in St Petersburg that was supposedly willing to run any lottery whatever, provided that the management could set the price of a ticket to participate.

What of the lottery in which a fair coin is tossed until it shows heads for the first time? If a head appears on the first toss, you win two roubles, but this amount is doubled each time a tail appears. The expected money value of this lottery—its long-run average payoff—is infinite.[3]

---

[2] Geoffrey Sayre-McCord's *Moral Philosophy* is a useful set of extracts from Hume's work that includes a brief autobiography he wrote on his deathbed. Also the text of Adam Smith's tribute.

[3] To find the expected value of something, you multiply each of its possible values by the probability that it occurs, and then sum all of these products. In the St Petersburg lottery, the

5.2. UTILITY

So should you be willing to liquidate your assets entirely in order to buy a ticket to participate? If so, you will have taken the risk of consigning yourself to poverty for a prospect that will return no more than eight roubles seven times out of eight.

The Bernoulli brothers proposed dealing with the problem by replacing the expected value of money by the expected value of the *utility* of money. Their idea is that the utility of an extra rouble paid to a billionaire is a lot smaller than the utility of an extra rouble to a beggar. If the utility of each extra rouble—the marginal utility of money—decreases fast enough, the St Petersburg Paradox disappears. The Bernoulli brothers guessed that the logarithm of money might serve as an adequate correlate of whatever the real utility of money may be to a person, but modern experiments have demolished any suggestion that such a simple answer might suffice.

Happiness. The founders of modern utilitarianism are usually said to be Jeremy Bentham and John Stuart Mill. They were hedonists in that they followed Aristotle and many others in regarding happiness as the target towards which humans should strive. For them utility was therefore to be identified with happiness. Nowadays, they are assumed to have thought that our brains incorporate biological meters that measure how much pleasure or pain we feel on a single scale like a barometer. We certainly feel pleasure and pain, but it is naive to imagine that we can model the mechanism in such a simple way.[4] However, it would be premature to pursue this point, since both Bentham and Mill have chapters to themselves.

Revealed preference. Bentham later registered his discomfort with identifying utility with happiness by observing that it would perhaps have been better if he had spoken of felicity rather than utility. What a pity he didn't! Even today, many philosophers are unaware that economists no longer follow their Victorian predecessors in identifying utility with happiness. The neoclassical orthodoxy does not even argue that economic behavior is caused by economic agents trying to maximize utility.

Neoclassical economics makes a virtue of assuming nothing whatever about what goes on in our heads. This is topic left for psychologists. The neoclassical theory of revealed preference applies whenever a person's choice behavior is sufficiently consistent. The choices can then be described by saying that they are chosen *as though* the person were maximizing the expected value of some abstract quantity.[5] Whatever this abstract quantity may be, economists call it utility.

So the theory does not say that consistent choices are necessarily made *because* people are maximizing their happiness, or anything else. This is the causal utility fallacy. We are able to attribute a utility function to them *because* their choice

---

expected value is therefore the sum of an infinite number of ones. For example, the probability that you win eight roubles in the St Petersburg lottery is one eighth, and eight times one eighth is one.

[4] *The Pursuit of Happiness* by Louis Narens and Brian Skyrms is an excellent survey of the long history of attempts to make the concept of happiness into something scientifically respectable. It is a pity that they did not extend their study to the attempts that continue to the present day.

[5] Many scholars contributed to this result, of which mention is made here only of Jimmy Savage who applied the final coat of polish in his *Foundations of Statistics*.

behavior is consistent. However, it does not follow that utility theory is necessarily at odds with maximizing happiness because maximizing happiness is one of the many ways that consistent choice behavior can be realized.

Insofar as the modern philosopher John Harsanyi is taken notice of it all, his use of the neoclassical theory of utility in sorting out the problems with utilitarianism left behind by Bentham and Mill is seldom distinguished from their psychological theory of utility. No wonder his work is not better appreciated!

5.3 Sympathy and Empathy

It is extraordinary that David Hume and his disciple Adam Smith seem to have been the first philosophers ever to have taken seriously the thought that empathy might be relevant to moral issues.[6]

Alice *empathizes* with Bob when she imagines herself in his shoes to see things from his point of view. If successful, she will then understand what his personal preferences are, but she will not necessarily *sympathize* with him, and so feel his joys and sorrows sufficiently strongly that they motivate her to some degree as they motivate him. For example, Alice might be a confidence trickster seeking to find what story will persuade Bob to part with his life savings.

Charlotte expresses an *empathetic preference* when she says that she would rather be Alice at the opera than Bob watching ice-hockey. We say this kind of thing all the time. It is understood to mean that Charlotte has imagined herself first in Alice's position, and then in Bob's, and prefers the former to the latter, although there is no way she can actually be Alice or Bob to check our how they feel about things.

Neither David Hume nor Adam Smith distinguished at all clearly between sympathetic and empathetic preferences. However, it is important to the ideas of both Richard Hare and John Harsanyi that they be firmly separated. Hutcheson would have found that their use of empathetic preferences fits nicely into his idea that personal and moral preferences live in separate worlds.

5.4 Convention

Hume's naturalism was much more thoroughgoing than Hutcheson's. He certainly did not subscribe to the idea that morality lives in a separate world from our everyday lives. He was particularly displeased with the invention of so-called Natural Laws like those of Locke. As he famously argued, such Natural Laws are actually artificial, and all that is natural about them is that it is natural that we should invent them. So why should we feel obliged to obey them? As Edmund Burke put it:

---

[6] Adam Smith attended Hutcheson's lectures as a student, but his real mentor was David Hume, who insisted that he not advertize this fact lest he become subject to the same censure that Hume had to endure.

5.4. CONVENTION

> Dark and inscrutable are the ways by which we come into the world. The instincts which gave rise to this mysterious process of nature are not of our making. But out of physical causes, unknown to us, perhaps unknowable, arise moral duties, which, as we are able perfectly to comprehend, we are bound indispensably to perform.

It is only with the advent of modern game theory that such dark and inscrutable mysteries have been laid open to the light of day. If a so-called Natural Law—albeit artificial—succeeds in coordinating behavior on an equilibrium in the game of life the citizens of a society play, then we do not need to seek supernatural reasons why we are obliged to obey it. Its strictures will be self-enforcing. All players will be optimizing according to their personal preferences provided the other players do the same.

David Hume used the word *convention* to describe the kind of rules that enforce themselves in this way. As Hume put it:

> Two men, who pull the oars of a boat, do it by an agreement or convention, though they have never given promises to each other. Nor is the rule concerning the stability of possession the less derived from human conventions, that it arises gradually, and acquires force by a slow progression, and by our repeated experience of the inconveniences of transgressing it. On the contrary, this experience assures us still more, that the sense of interest has become common to all our fellows, and gives us a confidence of the future regularity of their conduct: And it is only on the expectation of this, that our moderation and abstinence are founded. In like manner are languages gradually established by human conventions without any promise. In like manner do gold and silver become the common measures of exchange, and are esteemed sufficient payment for what is of a hundred times their value.

A reasonable response is to observe that rowing a boat is one thing, but sustaining a complex moral system as an equilibrium is another. But this problem disappears when the game of life being played has a repeated structure, because then the players can make use of the mechanism of reciprocity in sustaining an equilibrium. Hume understood this as well:

> I learn to do service to another, without bearing him any real kindness, because I foresee, that he will return my service in expectation of another of the same kind, and in order to maintain the same correspondence of good offices with me and others. And accordingly, after I have serv'd him and he is in possession of the advantage arising from my action, he is induc'd to perform his part, as foreseeing the consequences of his refusal.

Modern game theory has filled in the details of these insights of David Hume, but this is not the place to explain its theorems.[7] What is interesting here is why Hume's naturalism is almost unanimously rejected by moral philosophers, both of his time and of ours.

The reason is not hard to find. Moral philosophers are brought up in the rationalist tradition that Reason alone is adequate to deduce iron laws of morality

---
[7] My *Natural Justice* gives the arguments without getting mathematical.

that somehow bind us unconditionally. Are we to abandon this tradition in favor of the notion that the laws of morality are mere conventions, like whether we drive on the left or the right? The door is then open for the supposedly pernicious doctrine of moral relativism, in which everybody is said to make up their own morality for themselves!

In brief, the prejudices that closed so many doors to Hume during his lifetime are still active today in closing minds to his empirical solution to the dark and inscrutable problem of where morality comes from, and why citizens have a duty to honor the moral system that operates in their society.

Chapter 6
Beccaria

6.1 Crime and Punishment

Beccaria's widely read *Crimes and Punishments* of 1764 was the first serious attempt to propose a full-scale reform of the criminal justice system. It cries out against the brutality of the system in place all over Europe in his time—secret accusations, arbitrary verdicts, confessions obtained under torture, children hung for minor offences, compassion only for the rich and well-connected. Beccaria argues that a rational analysis should reject the eye-for-an-eye principle. Punishments should be set at the minimal level necessary to deter deviations from whatever social contract is in place.

Beccaria's book was important for utilitarianism because its deep concern for the plight of those at the bottom of the social heap opened hearts as well as minds to the need for social reform. When Jeremy Bentham later called for a society in which everybody should count for one, and nobody should count for more than one, people were willing to listen because the ground had been prepared by Beccaria and his followers.

6.2 Still Worth Reading

Why was Beccaria's book so successful? One reason is the calm rationality with which he expresses his utilitarian ideas for reform that makes the book still well worth reading today. The following sentence from the book's introduction is typical:

> If we look into history we shall find that laws, which are, or ought to be, conventions between men in a state of freedom, have been for the most part the work of the passions of a few, or the consequences of a fortuitous or temporary necessity; not dictated by a cool examiner of human nature ... with only this end in view, the greatest happiness of the greatest number.

It was not the custom in the eighteenth century to document your sources, but Beccaria would not have spoken of the greatest happiness of the greatest number if he had not read Hutcheson. He had also read Locke on the social contract, Helvétius on law enforcement, and Hume on conventions. In just a few pages, he wove their insights into an elegant synthesis that must have been a revelation to intellectuals of the time seeking an outlet for their dissatisfaction with the reactionary regimes in place all across Europe.

We can still learn from Beccaria's book. When living in California, I was shocked by the wide support for the 'three-strikes and you're out' law that mandated very heavy sentences for repeated offences—rationalized by the observation that 'people like us' don't need to steal a pizza. Beccaria ends his book with what he calls a theorem that still applies today:

> A punishment may not be an act of violence ... against a private member of society; it should be public, immediate, and necessary, the least possible in the case given, proportioned by the crime, and determined by the laws.

6.3 Enforcement

It is worth taking special note that Beccaria's legal experience leads him to endorse Helvétius in denying Shaftesbury's utopian aspirations that lead Godwin so far astray in the next chapter.

We cannot rely on the citizens of a society to put the public good before their own personal interests. We need the law to maintain our social contract. It is in the nature of the human species that self-interest sometimes leads citizens of a society to behave antisocially. Such antisocial acts or crimes need to be deterred by ensuring that the benefit derived from a crime is outweighed by the resulting punishment, which should be chosen to maximize the public good. Punishment will then cease to be out of all proportional to the severity of the crime. For example, hanging is not necessary to deter theft. Beccaria thought that fines would be an adequate disincentive for crimes against property.

6.4 Beccaria's Life and Times

Beccaria's (1738–1794) actual name was Cesare Bonesana. He inherited the title of Marchese di Beccarria from his father, who was a Milanese aristocrat of no great fortune. He seemed to have suffered from a bipolar temperament that was not improved by the "fanatical" Jesuit school to which he was sent at the age of eight. But he retained his independence of mind in spite an education that sought to suppress all human feeling. He showed some mathematical aptitude, but no hint was apparent of his gift for philosophy. Eventually, he graduated from the University of Pavia in 1758 with a degree in law.

His marriage to a girl of sixteen in 1761 led to a breakdown of relations with his father, who cut off his financial support for a while. But the marriage survived the poverty in which it began, and ultimately he was reconciled with his father when children began to appear. At that time, there was period of lively intellectual debate called the Milanese Enlightenment, in which Beccaria was active in the café society that developed in Milan in much the same way as in Paris or London. The publication of *Crimes and Punishments* eventually led to an invitation to meet with les philosophes who were still all the rage at that time in Paris. But his introversion proved an insuperable problem, and he returned to his wife and family in Milan after a few weeks.

Political economy? During this period, Beccaria wrote several pamphlets on political economy. A book *Elements of Public Economy* was published in 1804 after his death. As with John Stuart Mill and Henry Sidgwick, whose lives are coming up later, he is therefore credited with being a pioneer economist, but it cannot be said that he contributed anything particularly original to the foundations of the subject. However, he was enough of an economist to be appointed to a Chair of Law and Economy in 1768 that was founded in his honor by the Palatine College of Milan, where his lectures on economics echoed the views of the Scottish school that began with the economics essays of David Hume, and came to full fruition with Adam Smith's *Wealth of Nations*.

Success! Beccaria first published *Crimes and Punishments* anonymously for fear that expressing such reformist ideas would lead to his being persecuted by the Milanese government, but both Frederick the Great of Prussia and Catherine the Great of Russia endorsed his analysis in seeking to reform their own penal systems. Thomas Jefferson and John Adams quoted from it. Jeremy Bentham devoted a good deal of his life to proposing reforms to the English legal system partly in response to the book. But perhaps Beccaria's biggest success in his lifetime arose when the Grand Duchy of Tuscanny abolished the death penalty, citing *Crimes and Punishments* as its reason. Even the Milanese government finally endorsed his ideas, so that he was able to publish an edition bearing the name of its author.

Beccaria died in 1794—the same year that Robespierre went to the guillotine—but perhaps he never learned how the hopes for a better world that the French Revolution must have brought to reformers like himself were to be so badly disappointed.

Chapter 7
Godwin

7.1 Physician, Heal Thyself!

It is not Godwin's absurdly naive philosophy that is interesting. As a philosopher, he might be characterized as a real-life Candide attempting to fill the shoes of his mentor Pangloss in preaching that all can be for the best in this best of all possible worlds.[1]

What is interesting about Godwin is his seeming inability to learn that the utopian principles on which he mulishly organized his own ramshackle life do not work, so that he was forced further and further into hypocrisy to survive. How come he came to be regarded as a guru in his early years? What kind of society would allow such a threadbare prophet to be taken seriously? What is to be learned about the utopians of our own time, who similarly threaten our tranquility with their unworkable schemes?

Most of this chapter is about Godwin's life and times in an attempt to understand the phenomenon of utopianism. His life was certainly full of incident as his principles led him and his family further and further into debt and disgrace, but one cannot avoid feeling a good deal of affection for him. I even found myself smiling when he escaped spending his last few years in a debtors prison after mysteriously being awarded a pension by a Tory government that he had spent his life deriding.

7.2 Political Justice

William Godwin owed his very considerable reputation as a Victorian guru to his book *Political Justice*. The book argues, among much else, that "the end of virtue is to add to the sum of pleasurable sensations", so Godwin certainly counts as a utilitarian, although not one of whom Hutcheson would have approved.

Godwin tells us, "To a rational being there is but one rule of conduct: justice,

---
[1] Voltaire's *Candide* makes a mock of the philosopher Gottfried Leibniz by representing him in the person of the absurdly optimistic Dr Pangloss.

and one mode of ascertaining that rule: the exercise of his understanding." He thereby identifies himself as a rationalist, but the consequentialist conclusion to which he is led by applying his reason is nothing like the deontological Categorical Imperative of Immanuel Kant (1724–1804). According to Godwin's rationality:

> If justice have any meaning, it is just that I should contribute everything in my power to the benefit of the whole.

In Godwin's most famous example—without which he might have been forgotten altogether—you can rescue one of two folk from a fire: the saintly Archbishop Fénelon or his parlour maid. Godwin tells us that justice demands that you rescue the Archbishop because he contributes more to the public good, even if the parlour maid turns out to be your mother. He thereby ignores the standard idea—going back at least as far as Epicurus—that justice must be the same for everyone. Or as Jeremy Bentham put it, "Every man to count for one, and no one to count for more than one."

Godwin pursues his utopian instincts to the limit. If we were all to follow where Reason leads, governments would be superfluous, a necessary evil at best. So he is usually characterized as a political anarchist, alongside more serious figures like Kropotkin. But Godwin would have no truck with violence. So how to achieve the utopia that the reign of reason would bring to our suffering world? Proceed as though it were here already, and thereby promote the perfectability of the human species by influencing those with whom you interact!

So he did his best to do so. Always tell the truth, even if no harm would follow from telling a friend something nice about his awful poem. Marriage is a ball and chain, so let us put it aside, and encourage free love for all (although he seems to have retained his own virginity until seduced by Mary Wollstencraft rather late in life). Sponging off your friends is fine; they have the same duty to help you as you would have to save Archbishop Fénelon from the fire. But he was admittedly generous with his own small funds when his friends were threatened with the horrors of a Victorian debtors prison.

7.3 Godwin's Life

William Godwin (1756–1836) was born into a family of nonconformist ministers who lived on the breadline in the bleak fens of Cambridgeshire. He was a sickly child, one of thirteen brothers and sisters, of whom only six survived. Religion was a way of life in the fens, a harsh and unforgiving kind of Calvinism broken into mutually hostile shards that kept his father moving from one miserable living to another.

Dissenting minister. Godwin's talent was recognized insofar as he was educated to be a minister himself, but he was thought to be too pushy by both his family and his fellow scholars. The childhood he endured as a result was lonely. He filled its longeurs by writing religious tracts and sermons, together with a bunch of comedies and tragedies in verse on classical and religious themes.

7.3. GODWIN'S LIFE

Godwin's attempt to establish himself as a minister himself was a failure. It seems that he was too ready to do his own thinking for himself rather than fall in with the intolerant beliefs of the communities he sought to serve. It did not help that nonconformist heresies were ten-a-penny, each supposedly consigning their victims to an eternity of torment in the fires of Hell. Eventually his faith was suborned after first reading a tract of the Baron d'Holbach, and then the *De L'Esprit* of Helvétius. He then abandoned the ministry altogether in favor of life as a Grub Street author, whose hand-to-mouth existence is so eloquently described by Samuel Johnson.

Grub Street writer. He made what living he could writing whatever Grub Street booksellers would pay for. Parliamentary reviews and political pamphlets brought a small but steady income, but he also wrote trashy novels and unperformed plays—anything that might bring in some money. He could have lived a steadier life if he had been willing to become a political hack paid from party funds, but he kept his integrity in this respect.

In 1788, Godwin abandoned the religious convictions of his youth altogether. He described himself as a Deist in the style of les philosophes. The next year saw the Storming of the Bastille, and the big political question in London was what attitude should be taken to to the French Revolution. Edmund Burke took the negative view. The utopian idea that one can throw off the conventions developed over many years, and start from scratch with a brand-new constitution struck him as profoundly impractical. The predictions he offered in his *Reflections on the Revolution in France* about the future course of the revolution turned out to be depressingly accurate. But before things began to fall apart in Paris, William Godwin was an enthusiastic member of those calling for a similar revolution in London.

His invitation to a dinner given for Tom Paine by the publisher of his *Rights of Man*—a robust denial of Burke's book—gives some impression of his status at this time. Tom Paine's earlier *Common Sense* was credited with having sparked the American Revolution, and so Paine was a hero in revolutionary France. Apparently, he did not speak much at the dinner, and Godwin was forced to listen instead to Mary Wollstencraft, whose *Vindication of the Rights of Woman* is still regarded as one of the pioneer texts of the feminist movement. He changed his opinion of her later, as we shall see.

During this period, he worked hard on his *Political Justice*, which supposedly set down the philosophical principles for a peaceful revolution in Britain. The same year saw the publication of his novel *Caleb Williams*. These two works sold very well—not only solving his financial problems in the short term, but establishing him as a leading member of London's intellectual radical elite—an intimate of such literary figures as Samuel Coleridge, William Hazlitt, Charles Lamb and Richard Sheridan.

Jacobins take power in France. Events in France brought an end to the period in which the radical set of which Godwin was a part could seem to be leading the way forward. The Terror in which tens of thousands were butchered on the guillotine was not at all the peaceful road to a just society they had envisaged. Tom Paine—who had been enjoying the life of a revolutionary celebrity in Paris—

experienced the fate that moderates commonly suffer as revolutions are taken over by extremists. He found himself imprisoned for more than a year, narrowly escaping execution. The story goes that the chalk mark on the cell door of someone to be guillotined on a particular day was mistakenly marked on the inside of his door, which happened to be open while he received official visitors. So he survived until Robespierre himself was guillotined a few days later, after which his life was safe until his release was secured by James Monroe, the future US president.

The unexpected success of the French revolutionary armies was even more frightening than such stories of casual brutality. The British government turned to censorship and repression, supported by public opinion to a large extent. Those who had backed the French Revolution were now reviled and oppressed. Godwin never lost his guru status altogether, but his books were no longer guaranteed a wide readership, and he gradually declined into a genteel form of penury and debt that was made worse by his first ventures into sex at the age of forty or so.

Mary Wollstencraft. After her first meeting with Godwin at the dinner for Tom Paine, Mary Wollstencraft had moved to Paris to enjoy the freedoms promised at the dawn of the French Revolution. Through Paine, she became acquainted with the Girondins, who held power before the Jacobin coup. It must have been pleasant for her to find a milieu in which she was not patronized relentlessly for being female.

One of the utopian freedoms Godwin and others promised themselves in the anarchic paradise that they were about to achieve was free love. So when Wollstencraft fell in love with an American adventurer, she was free with her sexual favors in a manner that nearly all women at that time regarded as unacceptable. It all ended badly. She escaped the Terror, but found herself in London, the unmarried mother of a tiny baby, without any income when her publisher cut off her credit.

It is hard to disentangle the events that led to Wollstencraft and the virginal Godwin sharing a bed. My guess is that she shamelessly seduced him, but that he was a willing victim. Their future life together is captured by his needing to solicit a substantial loan of £50 for her from his friend Thomas Wedgewood.[2] A pregnancy followed, and they married secretly. It was against their utopian principles, but polite society would otherwise have punished their baby for being a bastard. However, when their marriage became known, it became evident that Wollstencraft had borne her previous baby out of wedlock, and so some of her polite friends severed their relationship with her. She died from complications in childbirth, but the baby Mary survived. She eventually eloped with the poet Shelley, and achieved fame as the author of *Frankenstein*, but right now Godwin was left with two small children to care for.

---

[2] Thomas Wedgewood was the son of Josiah Wedgwood, who made himself rich by producing elegant pottery. They were both utopian in their outlook, and could afford to to be generous in supporting utopian causes. Josiah is mostly remembered for his stout support of the anti-slavery movement, but he was also active alongside Robert Owen in founding utopian communes on socialist principles.

7.3. GODWIN'S LIFE

Another marriage. Godwin wrote a *Memoir* intended to honor Wollstencraft's intellectual efforts, but he told too much of the truth, and his reputation suffered among both her friends and her enemies. Things were made worse by the fact that Anti-Jacobinism was now in full swing in London. For Anti-Jacobins, the philosophy of Godwin and Wollstencraft was synonymous with atheism, treason, socialism and debauchery. Godwin's *Memoir* merely added fuel to the flames.

Godwin married a second time, after being seduced by a neighbor without much pretence at a courtship. She was on her beams ends with fatherless children of her own, and I guess he needed a mother for his children as much as she needed a father for hers. The marriage was no great success—she was as difficult as Wollstencraft but without much in the way of brains—but they soldiered on together, falling deeper and deeper into debt, as Godwin's writings brought in less and less, so that he was anxiously forced to juggle his loans, with money borrowed from Peter to pay back the overdue loan from Paul. They set up a children's bookshop, seeking to make ends meet, but it was always under-capitalized, and proved yet another burden in the end. This road they were following was leading inevitably to the debtors prison, but then Percy Bysse Shelley burst on the scene.

Frankenstein. Shelley was a teenage aristocrat when he wrote to Godwin, throwing himself at his feet. His flamboyant character and gift for poetry made him a suitable companion for the bad Lord Byron in later years. There was even the prospect of money in the background when he succeeded to his father's estates. Godwin sponged off him unmercifully from the beginning. His position was that Shelley had a duty to keep him afloat for the same reason that you should rescue Archbishop Fénelon before your mother.

With such a dashing young man in and out of the house, it was no wonder that Mary Godwin—Godwin's daughter with Mary Wollstencraft—was swept off her feet at the age of sixteen. They eloped together, taking with them Mary's older stepsister, and leaving behind Shelley's young wife, who eventually took her own life. This is perhaps the most shabby episode in Godwin's retreat from his fine principles. He still wrote whinging letters to Shelley explaining how justice demanded that he increase his subsidies, but trying unsuccessfully to stand clear of the accusation that he was pimping his daughter.

Godwin's ignoble attempt to exploit his daughter's elopement is eclipsed by her writing *Frankenstein* as part of a literary game she played with Shelley and Byron during a vacation in Switzerland. A ray of light in a miasma of hypocricy.

Death. Godwin died in 1836. His last few years were rendered tranquil by the award of a pension by a Tory government that had done its best to persecute him and other radicals during his years of fame, but had found the judicial system too robust to go along with the more extreme of their repressive measures. It is hard to guess what arguments were used to persuade the Tories then in power to subsidize someone they had once regarded as a dangerous radical. Could it be that Godwin's utopianism touched even their flinty hearts?

Chapter 8
Bentham

8.1 Bentham and Mill?

Who is the founder of modern utilitarianism? The general view confers this title on Jeremy Bentham, although his name is usually twinned with that of John Stuart Mill. The unspoken implication is that the eccentric Bentham may have hit upon the phrase "the greatest happiness for the greatest number", but it was Mill who was the serious thinker who provided utilitarianism with sound intellectual foundations.

We have seen that it is actually Francis Hutcheson who first spoke of the greatest happiness for the greatest number, but Bentham apparently did not read his work. Some authors have plausibly traced the origins of his ideas to Leibniz or Beccaria, but I see no reason to doubt his giving credit himself to Helvétius. However, I am more interested in separating his contributions to utilitarianism from those of Mill, whose life is the subject of the next chapter.

8.2 Termites and Moths

Isaiah Berlin is famous for separating philosophers into hedgehogs and foxes. In comparing Bentham and Mill, I propose a division into termites and moths.

Termites build from the ground up, mixing their saliva with mud to construct towers that rise far above their daily lives, but can never hope to reach the sky. The moths are attracted by the lights shining in the sky, and build castles in the air that embody their hopes to transcend our earthly lives. The termites say that the airy castles of the moths are held aloft by imaginary skyhooks. The moths say that nothing worthwhile can come of grubbing around in the mud.

One might criticize the termites by saying that they need to look up to see where their towers might reach. One might criticize the moths by saying that they need to look down to see that they are standing in the air.

Bentham a termite? The following quote places Bentham firmly among the termites:

> Nature has placed mankind under the governance of two sovereign masters, pain and pleasure. It is for them alone to point out what we ought to do, as well as to determine what we shall do. On the one hand the standard of right and wrong, on the other the chain of causes and effects, are fastened to their throne. They govern us in all we do, in all we say, in all we think: every effort we can make to throw off our subjection, will serve but to demonstrate and confirm it. In words a man may pretend to abjure their empire: but in reality he will remain subject to it all the while. The principle of utility recognises this subjection, and assumes it for the foundation of that system, the object of which is to rear the fabric of felicity by the hands of reason and of law.

As for the skyhooks of the moths, Bentham is famous for rejecting the notion of imprescriptible Natural Rights offered in the 1789 French Declaration of the Rights of Man as "nonsense upon stilts", but he was no less negative than Hume about all attempts to invent unnatural Natural Laws whether offered as Laws of Reason, Right Reason, Natural Justice, Natural Equity, Good Order, or anything else. He would have been equally unwilling to take seriously either the Natural Duty of John Rawls, or the Moral Commitment of John Harsanyi.

Popularity? The arbiters of fashion seldom care about foundational issues, and things were no different in Victorian times. In his novel *Hard Times,* Charles Dickens encapsulates his disdain for termites like Jeremy Bentham by representing him in the person of Mr Gradgrind, who tells little Louisa never to wonder: "By means of addition, subtraction, multiplication, and division, settle everything somehow, and never wonder." A N Wilson's *Victorians* brings this hostile attitude forward into the present day by applying the word *benthamite* to any economic development of which he disapproves, so that Bentham is simultaneously held responsible not only for all the crimes of authoritarian socialism, but also for the excesses of laissez-faire capitalism. In brief, the bright lights in the sky cannot be attained by building towers of mud. So towers of mud are unworthy of consideration.

Bentham did not help his image by being markedly eccentric. The continuing display of his mummified corpse in the foyer of University College London as specified in his will is the most obvious of his many oddities. His obsession with building a circular prison in which a warder placed at the center could simultaneously monitor the behavior of many prisoners is another. But it makes no sense to judge a creative genius by what we perceive as their follies. Otherwise it would be necessary to condemn Isaac Newton for his attempts to advance alchemy and numerology.

Mill a moth? Bentham was definitely a termite, but what of Mill? In spite of his heavy-handed literary style and philosophical commitment to naturalism, I think Mill was a moth.

Mill genuinely wanted to reform Victorian society, and saw that the hearts and minds of movers and shakers are not to be won by filling in the gaps left by Bentham in his tower of logic. Indeed, Bentham's atheism and lack of respect for the legal establishment discredited his own calls for reform from the outset. So he offered a version of utilitarianism more suited to the appetite of public intellectuals of the time, dazzled like Godwin by the bright lights in the sky, and unwilling to be held back by tiresome questions of why this should follow from that, or whether the sum of happiness is a genuinely meaningful concept.

One might capture the difference in their attitude to Bentham's observation that poetry is no better than the tavern game of push-pin as a source of pleasure. What other view is possible if every man is to count for one, and no one to count for more than one? But Mill thought that a cultivated person like himself knew better than the common man what was good for him, and the views of the nomenclatura to which he belonged should prevail.

Tower of Babel? My own view is that the continuing gulf between moths and termites in philosophy is largely unbridgeable, but that utilitarianism is an exception where bridges can be built. But the moths have to give up the idea that evolutionary ethics is piece of idle folly, and the termites have to give up the idea that the moths never get beyond mouthing utopian fairy stories. So I have vainly devoted part of my life to trying to build a tower of mud and saliva that reaches up from the materialism of Charles Darwin to the utopian aspirations of benign but impractical reformists like Godwin or Mill. My *Natural Justice* certainly does not have all the answers, but I think it demonstrates that such a tower is a possibility that needs to be taken seriously by both termites and moths. In any case, it explains why I am anxious to separate Bentham and Mill in exploring the origins of utilitarianism.

8.3 Bentham's Foundations

The idea that people can be adequately modeled as seekers of pleasure and avoiders of pain goes all the way back to Epicurus and beyond. Critics who regard such naturalistic foundations as inimical to their utopian aspirations have been so successful in discrediting such Epicurean foundations that the very word *epicurean* now denotes an orgy of gluttony and lust. But neither Bentham nor Epicurus were into orgies of any kind, although Bentham reportedly enjoyed a cup of hot chocolate along with plate of his favorite spiced ginger nuts.

The real Epicurus was in fact totally sold on the Socratic idea that the unexamined life is not worth living. He tells us that the tranquility obtainable through philosophical reflection is worth more than all that money can buy. When he reduces human motivation to pleasure or pain, he was distinguishing between what one might call instrumental and intrinsic preferences.[1]

An instrumental preference is one for which you can give a reason. Why do I prefer a hammer to a screwdriver? Because I want to drive a nail into a piece of wood. Why do I choose not to drink myself into oblivion? Because hangovers are awful. Why do I not fear death? Because when you are dead, you are not there to experience it. But you cannot go on asking why for ever. Some preferences are

---

[1] Economists speak of direct and indirect utilities. Something is assigned a direct utility if no reason need be given why an economic agent wants it. Something has an indirect utility if it is instrumental in gaining access to items that have been assigned a direct utility. When neoclassical economists quote the slogan *De gustibus, non est disputandum*, they are talking about direct utilities.

intrinsic. One cannot give a better reason for them than saying that I choose this rather than that because I like it. That is to say, pleasure and pain are what are left as explanatory variables when all the resources of philosophical reflection have been exhausted.

For Bentham, this reduction was important to his insistence that every man is to count for one, and no one to count for more than one—including the ignorant and the stupid. Their pleasure and pain needs to be counted as being no less worthy than those with educated and refined tastes. In arguing that pleasure and pain are fundamental, he was not denying that educated or refined tastes like his own are valuable, or that philosophical reflection in the Epicurean style cannot improve your life, he was simply trying to move to a level at which everybody could be treated as equal.

But how do we model how we experience pleasure and pain? Bentham proceeded as though we are equipped with a meter in our heads that measures how much pleasure or pain we feel on a single scale like a barometer. The idea that pain is simply negative pleasure finds no favor with modern neuroscientists, but it is surely a reasonable first stab at what continues to be a problem whose solution remains elusive. However, was it a good idea to call the reading on such a meter the *utility* of an experience, when the usefulness of something is surely an instrumental issue? Bentham himself had doubts on this issue, saying later that it would have been better to speak of *felicity* rather than *utility*. Nowadays, modern followers of this psychological line call themselves hedonic utilitarians. For them as for Mill, the word *happiness* refers the reading on Bentham's imaginary meter.

I guess that nobody denies that feeling happy or sad is a real thing, but I for one am doubtful that one can realistically tie these feelings down with a single number. My own view is that we would do better to follow John Harsanyi and other preference utilitarians in reinterpreting the word *utility* to mean what it means to modern neoclassical economists who rely on the theory of revealed preference, leaving the happiness interpretation of Bentham and Mill to their behavioral cousins to make of what they can. However, the rest of this chapter continues to speak of utility in the sense of Bentham and Mill.

Comparing utilities? To compute the sum of utilities in a society, it is necessary that we be able to compare the utilities of different people, but who says that such comparisons are meaningful? Until comparatively recently, it was a dogma in neoclassical economics that such comparisons make no sense at all. Bob may complain more than Alice in the dentist's chair, but is he really suffering more? Charlotte may argue that her appreciation of the music of Bach brings her more pleasure than is possible for Daniel listening to heavy metal rock, but without access to their imaginary internal pleasure meters, who can say one way or the other?

Bentham does not evade this interpersonal comparison problem:

> 'Tis vain to talk of adding quantities which after the addition will continue to be as distinct as they were before; one man's happiness will never be another man's happiness: a gain to one man is no gain to another: you might as well pretend to add 20 apples to 20 pears!

8.3. BENTHAM'S FOUNDATIONS

However, he steamrollers on, treating the assumption that this and various other problems mentioned below have solutions as axiomatic. With characteristic frankness, he observes "that which is used to prove everything, cannot itself be proved".

The props that termites erect to bridge gaps in their towers—like those left behind by Bentham—seem no different to moths than the skyhooks they invent themselves. They certainly feel no need to try to fill the holes. After all, what good is a tower if it does not seem to provide a solid foundation for their utopian reforms? So they ignored the gaps in his argument that Bentham confidently thought would be filled by his successors. In fact, more than a hundred years went by before the gaps were finally filled by John Harsanyi using the neoclassical interpretation of utility to model the notion of an empathetic preference first touted by David Hume and Adam Smith.

Fictitious Postulatum? Suppose we have found some way of measuring Alice and Bob's happiness so that one unit of happiness for Alice can be regarded as being worth the same as one unit of happiness for Bob. Why then should the sum of their individual happinesses be taken to be the happiness of their little society? Why not, for example, their product?[2]

Bentham has no answer to this problem either. It is a necessary assumption—a fictitious postulatum—without which all reasoning is at a stand.[3] Again the world had to wait for John Harsanyi for an answer, although the insurance argument that he employed had been proposed a long time earlier by the much undervalued Francis Edgeworth in 1881.

Missionaries and Cannibals. Bentham often gets the blame for the heartless aspect of utilitarianism captured by a story about missionaries and cannibals.

Ten missionaries are held at bay by cannibals, and offered their freedom if they turn over one their number to be cooked and eaten. If suitable utilities are assigned to the various possibilities, utilitarianism will then sometimes recommend the sacrifice of one of the missionaries because his loss is outweighed by the gain of his companions. An alternative telling of this fable was mentioned in the chapter on Helvétius. There an eye could be surgically removed from a sighted person and implanted in a blind person.

This accusation is somewhat unfair, as Bentham clearly shared the egalitarian

---

[2] The product is in fact sometimes seriously advanced as an alternative to the sum, as documented in Narens and Skyrms' *Pursuit of Happiness*. One might, for example, take the utility of happiness to be its logarithm, as the Bernoulli brothers suggest for money. Maximizing the sum of utility would then be the same as maximizing the product of happiness. This would be a mistake for the same reason that it is a bad idea to interpret the Nash bargaining solution as a fairness criterion. Using the product makes interpersonal comparisons irrelevant. But how can fairness judgements be made if you cannot tell whether one person has ended up better off than another?

[3] Part of Bentham's charm is his delight in inventing new words or phrases. The words *maximum* and *minimum* are examples of a whole range of technical terms we owe to him. We even owe him the word *utilitarian*. But sometimes his neologisms are decidedly eccentric, as with his will referring to his embalmed corpse as an *auto-icon*. He similarly called his design for a circular prison the *Panopticon*, which cannot have helped his determined but ultimately unsuccessful attempts to gain government finance for the project.

instincts of the critics who charge him with being heartless. Bentham repeatedly argues that the principle of utility will tend to generate equitable distributions of economic surpluses. The following quote is typical:

> The less unequal the distribution of the external instruments of felicity is—the greater, so security be unshaken, will be the sum of felicity itself.

This is certainly correct when money is to be split between two identical individuals, provided that their marginal utility for money decreases in the manner that Bentham was perhaps the first to describe when he wrote that "the quantity of happiness produced by a particle of wealth will be less and less at every particle". But Bentham seems to have believed that maximizing total utility will generate equal outcomes over a much larger domain than modern analysts would accept. Not that he overlooked altogether the fact that his principle of utility will sometimes call for the sacrifice of the few for the sake of the many, but one has to search his writings with a toothcomb for a suitable reference. But what if he had appreciated the full extent to which utilitarianism implies unequal outcomes? What if he had been able to read Rawls' *Theory of Justice?* Would the inventor of the "addibility of happiness" then have been shaken in his convictions?

8.4 Bentham's Life

Jeremy Bentham (1748–1832) was born to a well-off family in London. His father was a successful lawyer, who was able to buy him a fancy education that brought him to Oxford at the age of twelve. But he was left with a distaste for the academic life—colleges are of seats of privilege, prejudice and idleness—and a deep distrust of establishment values.

He embarked on a legal career, and was called to the bar in 1769, but abandoned practising law after only one case. After reading of the utility principle in the works of David Hume, he devoted his life to advocating reform across the board. He was wholeheartedly against censorship, slavery, and capital punishment. He was for the separation of church and state, equal rights for women, and the civilized nurturing of children.

In spite of his personal eccentricity, and his attacks on the legal traditions endorsed by Blackstone,[4] he was seriously effective on the legal front, eventually becoming famous for the constitutions he provided on demand. If Simon Bolivar had ever managed to create the superstate in South America he worked for so hard, its constitution would have been written by Jeremy Bentham. Bentham even offered to rewrite the American constitution for President James Madison in 1811, but Madison was unsurprisingly satisfied with the constitution he already had.

Bentham was not very systematic in getting his work published. I mention here only his *Introduction to the Principles of Morals and Legislation*, and the delightful *Anarchical Fallacies*. However, scholars have no lack of data, for he left behind enormous quantities of manuscript, which will eventually be published in

---

[4]Blackstone was the Victorian authority on why law—especially the law on property—is supposedly not just a bunch of conventional compromises as proposed by David Hume.

some eighty volumes by the Bentham project at University College London. I have seen some of the manuscripts. I found the handwriting totally illegible, but it is apparently not so hard to transcribe after one has got used to his style.

Bentham was proud of being regarded as one of the founders of UCL, famously described by Thomas Arnold as "that godless institution in Gower Street" because it practised religious toleration. However, Bentham was only its spiritual father, in spite of the mural under UCL's landmark rotunda showing him receiving UCL's charter. Bentham's will specified that his corpse be stuffed and mounted, so that he could always chair meetings of the UCL governors. Nowadays, his corpse—his auto-icon—is kept on display in a glass cabinet. I sat next to it once as a guest at a dinner of the Jeremy Bentham Society.[5]

Bentham's personal life does not seem to have been very happy. He described himself in old age as a hermit, and is reported to have become tearful on occasion of the opportunities he let slip by in his youth of contracting a loving marriage. I have heard it said that he must have had gay tendencies because he was often surrounded by young men anxious to join his reformist enterprise. I have heard similar things said of David Hume. But I think that both probably lived sexless lives. Godwin at least escaped the same fate.

8.5 Bentham's Unfinished Agenda

Jeremy Bentham's brutal honesty leaves termites like myself with a series of unanswered questions that will serve as a framework in evaluating the contributions of the utilitarians still to be considered.

- How is utility measured?
- How are the utilities of different people to be compared?
- Why add the utilities of different people?
- Why should I maximize the sum of utilities rather than my own?

Bentham is not usually thought to differ from Hutcheson and Godwin on this last point, but his lifelong concern with using utilitarian principles to motivate practical reforms in the British legal system seems to me to place him closer to the alternative view of Helvétius—that utilitarianism needs to be interpreted as an instrument of public policy to be enforced by a benign government. It is a pity that he seems to have felt no need to emphasize the need to separate the interpretation of utilitarianism as a system of personal morality from its interpretation as an instrument of public policy. The subject was certainly a hot potato, both then and now, but it is hard to believe that Jeremy Bentham would deliberately fudge any issue at all.

---

[5]In those days, I was one of the many successors to David Ricardo—whose chair in Political Economy gave UCL the first Economics Department ever created anywhere (a claim disputed by the University of Glasgow on account of Adam Smith's holding their Chair of Moral Philosophy at an earlier date). David Ricardo is of independent interest for being an unusually hard-headed utopian socialist of the kind mentioned in the chapter on Godwin.

Chapter 9
Mill

9.1 Successor to Bentham

John Stuart Mill is referred to by both his forenames to distinguish him from his father, James Mill, who moved to London from Edinburgh in 1802, where he became a close associate and aide of Jeremy Bentham, and a prominent member of London's set of philosophical radicals.

Hothouse radical When delivered of a son, James Mill decided that he would be shaped to be the leader of the next generation of radicals, beginning with Greek at the age of three. At the age of twelve, he was proficient not only in the classics, but in mathematics and history as well. At the age of fifteen, he was already writing works on philosophy and government. All this was achieved under the strict daily supervision of his father, with the result that his son grew up stunted as a human being in many ways—without the sparkle that can make youth such a delight, and subject to spiritual malaise in later life. But his father was successful in turning his son into very learned radical, a naturalist without any religious belief, and a true believer in the utilitarian ethos. All this is recounted from his point of view in John Stuart Mill's *Autobiography*, which is a fascinating read.

Leading philosopher? The adult John Stuart Mill (1806–1873) is sometimes said to be the leading philosopher of the nineteenth century in the English-speaking world—not just for his famous books *Utilitarianism* and *On Liberty*, but for his contributions to logic, mathematical philosophy and political economy. He certainly wrote a great deal on these latter subjects, but to what real effect?

As a one-time economist myself, I made several attempts to read his 1848 *Principles of Political Economy*, but its insuperable dullness got the better of me each time. I do not think he had any lasting influence in economics at all, and very little in mathematics or logic. On the other hand, he was genuinely effective in promoting the liberal doctrines that he inherited from his father, and from Jeremy Bentham—for whom he worked as an unofficial secretary from time to time. He was particularly eloquent on equality for women, and deserves to be numbered among the angels for his insistence that everybody should be free to say and do what they want to say and do, provided they do not infringe the freedom others to do the same. On the other hand, his paternalistic belief that it can be moral to lie to the masses "for their own good" is not something with which I am at all comfortable.

Career. John Stuart Mill was elected to the British House of Commons, but never held a university appointment. He worked for most of his life for the East India Company which ran British India in those days. One cannot help but feel that his benign form of paternalism would have made him ideal as a governor of some quiet corner of the British Empire, but he lived instead a life in London that cannot have been very happy. However, he found comfort in mixing not only with philosophical radicals, but with poets of the romantic movement that was all the rage in those days. He got on particularly well with Samuel Coleridge, whose seems to have been loved by everybody he met until they got to know him better. However, Mill's success in stepping outside the path laid down for him by his father was eclipsed when he fell hopelessly in love with Harriet Taylor, whom he met in 1830 at a dinner party.

Scandal? Unfortunately, Harriet Taylor was married to someone else, but her husband did not object to their meeting occasionally. There was talk of adultery, but Mill's protestations that their relationship was entirely platonic seem believable to me. Nevertheless, the perceived scandal cost Mill a number of friends. They married in 1851, two years after the death of her husband.

Harriet Taylor was cast in the mould of Mary Wollstencraft, and there seems no reason to doubt Mill's crediting her with being the inspiration, not only of his *Subjugation of Women*, but also of many of the other ideas in his later books. She died in 1858 in Avignon. Mill bought a house near the cemetery where she was buried, and lived there relatively quietly until his death in 1873.

9.2 Utilitarianism and Liberty

Judged by the standards of a philosophical moth, both Mill's *Utilitarianism* and his *On Liberty* are great successes. They provide persuasive skyhooks for a whole range of reforms, whose worth nobody thinks to challenge any more. We have good reason to be grateful to Mill for being a leader in promoting a whole range of improvements in both our civil liberties, and our attitudes to social justice. However, I shall focus here on his failure as a termite. What did he contribute to the unanswered foundational questions left behind by Bentham? Nothing at all.

Happiness. Mill is often credited with providing the intellectual foundations for utilitarianism left hanging in the air by the rude and eccentric Bentham. In *Utilitarianism*, these foundations consist of a chapter devoted to the proposition that what people want is happiness. But Mill's happiness is not the grubby happiness of pleasure-minus-pain attributed to lechers and gluttons. There are higher and lower pleasures, and the former are to be valued above the latter—a much easier sell than Bentham's crude rantings about reducing everything to bare-bones fundamentals.

But who decides by how much poetry is to be valued above push-pin? What criteria do these gurus employ once we have stepped beyond some crude measuring of pleasure and pain? We are not told. Why should we maximize the sum of everybody's happiness rather than our own? We are told only that, if happiness is what individuals want, then the sum of everybody's happiness must be what society wants. So, instead of Bentham's blunt admissions that his axioms are offered without proof, we are provided with a fuzzy intellectual blanket within which to wrap our prejudices while still calling ourselves utilitarians.

Liberty. Mill's *On Liberty* is an admirable defense of the kind of liberty we take for granted nowadays, but it is used here only to illustrate how Mill's approach to measuring utility differs from Bentham's.

Mill urges that liberty be valued for its own sake—that it is an intrinsic source of utility. Those of us who value our liberty are therefore supported by the utility principle. Bentham would have agreed that individual liberty is valuable, and that its promotion is supported by the utility principle, but not that liberty is valuable for intrinsic reasons.

Here is the trivial argument why liberty is valuable for instrumental reasons. We do not know what choices await us in the future—what the feasible sets will be from which we will seek to make an optimal choice. It is therefore in our interests that these feasible sets not be artificially constrained. But such a concern for liberty—although of great importance—is instrumental rather than intrinsic. We need not write liberty directly into what we count as utility because people seeking to maximize what we do count as utility will automatically favor their future feasible sets being free of unnecessary constraints. But who wants to listen to such fundamentalist ranting, when the whole subject can be brushed under the carpet simply by failing to distinguish between what economists call direct and indirect utilities?

9.3 Mill's Obituary of Bentham

I am sure that John Stuart Mill had no evil intentions in writing an assessment of Jeremy Bentham after his death that drew a parallel between Bentham and Samuel Coleridge, whose childish attempts at philosophy were no match for his gift for poetry. However, this assessment set in stone what still remains the modern view of Bentham: a minor celebrity in his time, but not a philosopher of the first rank.

Mill was particularly exercised by Bentham's refusal to be influenced by the school of German idealists, who were philosophically fashionable in England at that time. But it seems to me that, in such passages, Mill criticises Bentham for not being subject to his own weaknesses. After all, how can one follow up the insights of the Scottish Enlightenment as represented by David Hume, and simultaneously give credence to the categorical denials of this approach embraced by Immanuel

Kant? Such fudging was totally alien to Bentham, who did all his own thinking for himself, and followed the logic wherever it led, however unpopular or unfashionable his conclusions might prove to be.

But we must make allowances for Mill's stolen childhood. My guess is that Mill never forgave Bentham for being the mentor and friend of his domineering father.

Chapter 10

Jevons

Modern economists do not take John Stuart Mill seriously as one of their founding fathers. William Jevons was the first serious economist to take up the Victorian concept of utility as envisaged by Bentham and Mill, and use it in a systematic way to obtain results that are still valued today.

I do not think Jevons can be said to be a utilitarian himself if the term is taken to mean determinedly seeking the greatest happiness for the greatest number, although he was certainly a fellow traveller. He nevertheless gets a chapter to himself because his story provides an opportunity to tell how utilitarianism became totally discredited among neoclassical economists in the 1930s.

10.1 Cardinal Utility?

Jevons made the utility concept of Bentham and Mill into a working tool for economic modeling, but contributed nothing to Bentham's unfinished agenda. He simply accepted Bentham's axiomatic foundations, as in the following quote:

> Pleasure and pain must be regarded as measured upon the same scale, and as having, therefore, the same dimensions, being quantities of the same kind, which can be added and subtracted.

However, Jevons was definitely a termite, in that he built a tower of logical inference on these foundations that is nowadays referred to as *classical* economic theory—as opposed to the *neoclassical* theory by which it was eventually displaced.

Marginal utility. The classical theory of utility takes for granted that economic agents come equipped with an internal *cardinal* utility meter, which implies that utility is something that can be measured like temperature on a graduated scale. Jevons pointed out that what really matters in economics is seldom the actual reading on such a utility meter, but the amount by which it changes when the good whose utility is being measured goes up or down by some small amount—its marginal utility.

Decreasing marginal utility. Mathematicians will recognize marginality as a discrete correlate of the derivative of utility in the continuous case, and so understand how Jevons was able to use the differential calculus to obtain his results. In doing so, Jevons exploits the fact that the marginal utility of a good usually falls as the amount of the good increases, although priority for this claim is assigned to Hermann Gossen. (It is the first of his three laws.) But we have already seen that both Jeremy Bentham and the Bernoulli brothers already had the idea before any professional economists were involved. As Bentham put it:

> The quantity of happiness produced by a particle of wealth will be less and less at every particle.

Marginalist revolution. Later economists—notably Alfred Marshall—realized that the use of marginality arguments makes it possible to dispense with cardinal utility altogether when studying markets. Neoclassical economics is therefore marked by the Marginalist Revolution in which the dubious assumption that we all come equipped with meters that measure our happiness on a graduated scale is abandoned.

Under the new regime, only *ordinal* utility scales were permitted, which implies that no meaning can be attached to the gradations on the scale on which utility is measured. One can say that Alice or Bob would rather have an apple than a pear if their utility for an apple exceeds their utility for a pear, but their utilities cannot be used to say *by how much* he or she prefers an apple to a pear. Utilitarianism then has the ground cut from under its feet. How can we seek the greatest happiness for the greatest number if it is meaningless to say how much good a reform will generate for Alice compared with Bob?

Chicago School. The new wisdom became associated with an influential school of economists in Chicago. They swept the floor so thoroughly with their rivals that it became possible to argue, not just that the new foundations were better than the old because they assumed less, but that the old foundations are philosophically untenable. In particular, that it is literally impossible to compare Alice's welfare with Bob's. So welfare economics—and utilitarianism in particular—is an empty enterprise.

Pareto efficiency. Neoclassical textbooks of the period went so far as to define social optimality to mean nothing more than Pareto efficiency, named in honor of the Italian sociologist Vilfredo Pareto (1848–1923).

Something is Pareto efficient if nobody can be made better off without making somebody else worse off, which sounds fine until it is realized that Pareto efficiency takes no account of fairness at all. If a cake is to be shared between Alice and Bob, it is Pareto efficient that the whole cake be assigned to Alice because Bob cannot be given more without Alice getting less.

But the economists of the Chicago School were untroubled in throwing away the concept of fairness, because their new philosophical position on cardinality allowed their unbridled enthusiasm for markets to be expressed without any restraint at all. Since perfectly competitive markets generate Pareto-efficient outcomes, their position was that there is no need to consider any other way of distributing goods.[1]

Modern utilitarians need to be aware that the influence of the Chicago School is not yet dead—it is implicit whenever an appeal is made to Adam Smith's invisible hand. Economic textbooks sometimes still repeat the Chicago mantra that fairness and efficiency are incompatible by repeating an argument that makes sense only in perfectly competitive markets. Even the Chicago claim that utilitarianism is just a quaint survival from Victorian times still echoes down the dusty corridors of academe.

Von Neumann and Morgenstern utility. Lionel Robbins was the economic guru at the London School of Economics when I was hired there. He was famous for his jeremiads denouncing the very notion that cardinal utility could make sense. These jeremiads continued for at least twenty years after John von Neumann and Oskar Morgenstern had provided a perfectly respectable foundation for assuming cardinality. Robbins probably never caught up with the fact that his younger colleagues had abandoned the idea that cardinal utility is nonsense as soon as they had taken in the implications of von Neumann and Morgenstern's work.

However, the story of how von Neumann and Morgenstern's reinvention of utility theory reversed the attitudes of neoclassical economists to cardinal utility will have to wait until the chapter on John Harsanyi. Right now it is perhaps enough to say that the extreme views of the Chicago School are no longer taken seriously by economists. Even utilitarianism is acceptable to the modern generation of neoclassical economists, although they have yet to shake off their reputation as mean-minded, money-grubbing misfits inherited from the Chicago School.

10.2 Jevon's Life

William (Stanley) Jevons (1835–1882) was born to well-off parents, but his father's business went bankrupt, and he was forced to interrupt his education in the natural sciences to take up a position as Metallic Assayer to the Mint in far-off Sydney, Australia. Five years later, he and his wife were back in England, where he resumed his education at University College London. He is the fourth of our characters with a connection to UCL. Eventually, he became Professor of Political Economy at UCL in succession to David Ricardo. But his health was bad, and he suffered from depression. He resigned his position in 1880, and drowned two years later while bathing in the sea.

Jevon's reputation is based on his 1862 *General Mathematical Theory of Political Economy*, but he sought to be more than an economist, contributing works

---

[1] Actually, very few markets can be said to be *perfectly* competitive in the sense necessary to guarantee that Adam Smith's invisible hand will generate Pareto efficiency. One needs very large numbers of small buyers and sellers. Preferences need to be convex. Goods need to be infinitely divisible. And so on. But although the Chicago School downplayed these restrictions, nobody nowadays seriously denies that well-conducted markets work exceedingly well compared with the socialist alternatives that are constantly being revived.

throughout his life on topics in the natural sciences, as well as philosophy and logic. He was a life-long Unitarian, who inherited the reformist convictions of the sect.[2] So he worked in a practical way on behalf of the Victorian movement for self-improvement among the working classes. We would find him unacceptably patronizing in his attitude to social class, race and sex, but I do not think he left behind any statues in need of being toppled.

He would perhaps have been more effective as a utilitarian termite if he had not fallen prey to Herbert Spencer's teleological misunderstanding of Darwin's theory of evolution, which was all the rage in those days. His foundations certainly dispense with skyhooks. Goodness is not part of the natural universe, but is an artificial virtue. Economic theory can be used to study its inevitable development from primitive origins to something that can improve all our lives if it is extended to take account of sympathies, feelings and duties in the style proposed by David Hume and Adam Smith. But we must keep our feet on the ground. Charity is to be encouraged, but we must not lose sight of the fact that too much charity may endanger the creation of wealth.

10.3 Summary

In brief, William Jevons was an important step on the way from the naive theory of happiness of Bentham and Mill to the neoclassical theory of utility to which economists subscribe today. He is commonly said to be a utilitarian for this reason, but he was no more a utilitarian than David Hume according to the definition used in this book.

---

[2]Unitarians are Christians who deny the Trinity. Isaac Newton was one of their number.

Chapter 11
Sidgwick

11.1 Termite or Moth?

It is hard to classify Henry Sidgwick. He certainly had the instincts of a termite, as in the following quote:

> I have thought that the predominance in the minds of moralists of a desire to edify has impeded the real progress of ethical science: and that this would be benefited by an application to it of the same disinterested curiosity to which we chiefly owe the great discoveries of physics.

It is perhaps for this reason that his exposition of the late Victorian philosophical position on utilitarianism has been so widely admired by modern philosophers, notably John Rawls, who is fulsome in his praise. One might perhaps say that Sidgwick inspired Rawls—who is the subject of the next chapter—to bridge the gap between termites and moths more successfully than he was able to manage himself.

The Good? Why did Rawls make progress where Sidgwick faltered? Rawls would doubtless have said that he stood on the shoulders of a giant. But I think one must also take account of the intellectual climate of Sidgwick's time. Who was going to listen to someone who was not respectful of both the religious prejudices of the late Victorians, and their enthusiasm for Immanuel Kant and the German idealists?

This is perhaps the reason that Sidgwick's *Methods of Ethics* is so tolerant of the various skyhooks proposed by the three types of philosophical moths it considers, ultimately endorsing the ultimate of all skyhooks, namely that the Good is an "unanalyzable" notion without which all reasoning is at a stand. As the philosopher Moore put it, "If I am asked, 'How is Good to be defined?' my answer is that Good is Good and that is the end of the matter."[1] But how can one find foundations for a concept that is devoid of foundations by definition?

---

[1] Moore's Naturalistic Fallacy denies that the Good can be defined in naturalistic terms. All he offers in defense of this skyhook is that one can always ask of any proposed naturalistic definition: But is that really what the Good is? One might as well argue that the girl with the golden hair cannot be Alice, because one can always ask whether she is really Alice, and not some other girl.

11.2 What Kind of Hedonism?

Sidgwick is important in the development of utilitarianism for being unwilling to brush the enforcement question of why people ought to be utilitarians under the carpet. In addressing this issue, he distinguishes between psychological hedonism and ethical hedonism.

Psychological hedonism says that people act in their own self-interest. Ethical hedonism says that they act in the interest of society as a whole. Sidgwick criticized both Bentham and Mill for trying to have it both ways. How can it be consistent to argue that people ought to sacrifice their own interest for the public good, and simultaneously maintain that everyone actually looks after their own individual interests? But Sidgwick does not resolve this conflict between psychological hedonism and ethical hedonism. He tells us instead that there is a "dualism of practical reason".[2]

We have already commented on this fudge. Hutcheson and Godwin are both ethical hedonists. Harsanyi is another. Bentham and Mill somehow contrive to have a foot in both camps. Hume is a psychological hedonist, although willing to extend the notion to the idea that people are not always brutally selfish, but sympathize to some extent with the concerns of others. However, one cannot expect Alice to sacrifice much for Bob if he is an unknown stranger living in some far-off place.

Punishment. Only Helvétius offers a solution to the problem. He denies that ethical hedonism should be regarded as a rival to psychological hedonism. People can be psychological hedonists, but nevertheless support ethical hedonism as a policy to be enforced by a benign government.

The important word here is *enforcement*. We cannot rely on people's good nature to behave selflessly. Only saints would pay their taxes in full if they had any other option. The utopianism of Hutcheson and Godwin is hopelessly unrealistic, Even Mill recognized the need for some measure of compulsion when he wrote:

> For such actions as are prejudicial to the interests of others, the individual
> is accountable, and may be subjected to social or legal punishment.

Beccaria, of course, had long since been urging the use of utilitarianism in optimizing the scale of such punishments.

It is, in fact, the Helvétian view that has won out as far as practical applications of utilitarian principles are concerned. I do not suppose the economists who currently design our income tax schedules think about utilitarianism very much, or that they have ever heard of Helvétius, but to quote John Maynard Keynes, "Practical men, who believe themselves to be quite exempt from any intellectual influences, are usually slaves of some defunct economist." In this case, the defunct economist is the tax-farmer Helvétius.

---

[2] Kant distinguishes between pure and practical reason. Pure reason determines our beliefs. Practical reason determines our actions.

11.3 Sidgwick's Life and Times

Henry Sidgwick (1838–1900) was born to an undistinguished but well-off family, but found his way eventually into an elevated social circle that included Arthur Balfour, the current Prime Minister, who married his sister. After Sidgwick's death, Balfour offered the following tribute:

> Of all the men I have known he was the readiest to consider every controversy and every controversialist on their merits. He never claimed authority; he never sought to impose his views; he never argued for victory; he never evaded an issue.

One cannot, of course, speak ill of the recently dead, but other evidence suggests that Balfour was simply giving voice to the general good opinion in which Sidgwick was held by his contemporaries. He was, for example, elected to the secret society of Apostles when an undergraduate in Cambridge.[3] He spent the rest of his life as a popular fellow of Trinity College—perhaps the most prestigious of the Cambridge colleges—apart from a period when he chose to resign because he had come to doubt the formal religious requirements to which fellows were supposedly committed.

Methods of Ethics. Sidgwick's fame rests on his *Methods of Ethics*, which remains worth reading because of its critical assessment of the various ways of thinking about ethics that were fashionable at the time.

I personally do not value his attempts to defend utilitarianism because they are clouded both by the religious convictions that he abandoned only slowly during his life, and also by his willingness to embrace the rationalist skyhooks of the school of Geman idealists—notably Immanuel Kant—that the late Victorians thought offered a way to transcend the humdrum naturalism of the Scottish Enlightenment.

Nor am I convinced by the standard claim that he made important contributions to political economy. Indeed, insofar as he was at odds with his colleague Arthur Marshall on economic issues, history has sided with Marshall all down the line.

Summary. Sidgwick is perhaps best seen as a more polished, and better connected version of John Stuart Mill. This includes his major contributions to practical reform.

But I want to return at last to the conflict I see between his instincts as a termite and his flourishing as a moth. He was understandably dissatisfied with Immanuel Kant's metaphysical reasoning that the human soul is necessarily immortal.[4] He therefore sought experimental evidence by taking part in the ongoing investigations into the claims of spiritualists that were all the rage in late Victorian times. But, unlike his credulous colleagues in this enterprise, he was not easily deceived. He

---

[3] Russell and Moore are other famous Apostles. Russell's life gives the lie to the suggestion that the society was merely a gay club rather than a forum for intellectual debate. Biographies of Sidgwick similarly suggest that he was a suppressed homosexual himself, but who cares?

[4] The summum bonum (perfect good) is only possible on the supposition of the soul's immortality, because the Moral Law determines the Will of a man, and in his Will the perfect harmony of the mind with the Moral Law is the supreme condition of the summum bonum.

was particularly active in exposing the fraudulent claims of Madame Blavatsky and the Theosophical movement. What a pity that he did not bring the same scientific rigor to exposing the emptiness of the skyhook industry!

Chapter 12

Edgeworth

12.1 Irish Polymath

Francis Edgeworth was an Irish polymath who represents a last flowering of the Victorian enthusiasm for utilitarianism as a system of personal morality. His career as an economist bridges the transition from classical economics to neoclassical economics discussed in the chapter on Jevons.

Felicific calculus. Edgeworth's earlier work on utilitarianism might be characterized as teasing out the details of what Bentham called the felicific calculus—who should get what when utilitarian principles are applied—using mathematical methods that would have been beyond the comprehension of philosophers of his time.[1]

His later work leads him to be credited as one of the pioneers of the neoclassical enterprise that culminated in the Chicago School, whose ethos led to the neglect of utilitarianism by philosophers of economics for some fifty years. But Edgeworth would have disavowed this development. His exploration of the implications of using utilitarian principles to determine fair systems of taxation survived the influence of the Chicago School, and remains one of the foundational pillars of modern welfare economics.

The insurance argument. Edgeworth was certainly a termite, but he did not contribute to Bentham's unfinished agenda accept in one particular: Why sum the utilities of the individual citizens of a society to obtain the utility of society as a whole? On this subject, he is credited with being the originator of the insurance argument for utilitarianism. To paraphrase the more down-to-earth William Vickrey, who independently reinvented the idea some fifty years later:[2]

---

[1] His "Hedonical Calculus" *Mind* 4 (1879), 394–408 even employs the Calculus of Variations.
[2] In "Measuring Marginal Utility by Reactions to Risk" *Econometrica* 13 (1945), 319–333.

> To maximize the aggregate of utility over the population is equivalent to choosing that distribution of income which an individual would select if asked which economy he would like to join if he had an equal chance of landing in the shoes of each member of it.

Ideal Observers? But who is doing the choosing in Vickrey's version of the insurance argument? In this context and elsewhere, philosophers answer this question by inventing various personalized skyhooks generally called Ideal Observers. Adam Smith calls his an Impartial Spectator. Henry Sidgwick called his the Point of View of the Universe, a proposal seconded by the modern philosopher Peter Singer. Richard Hare refers to his ideal observer as an Archangel in the next chapter. Such inventions leave the problem of enforcement unresolved. Why should we honor the choice of an Ideal Observer—however impartial—rather than our own?

Helvétius would perhaps have chosen his Ideal Observer to be one of the allegorical statues of Justice with which we decorate our courts of law. The blindfold indicating her impartiality is echoed in the veil of ignorance introduced by Rawls in the chapter after next. Her standard of interpersonal comparison is represented by the scales she holds aloft in one hand, as pursued in the chapter on Harsanyi that comes after that. But the immediate point is the sword she flourishes in her other hand, which represents the power of government to enforce whatever its system of justice may be.

We have already reviewed Helvétius's invoking the power of government as a solution to the enforcement problem in the chapter devoted to him. It may seem unphilosophical for him to follow Thomas Hobbes in observing that "covenants without the sword are but words", but Helvétius would reply that real swords actually work, whereas the metaphysical skyhooks that utopians seek to substitute are no better than smoke and mirrors.

12.2 Fair Taxation

Although Edgeworth does not seem to have been influenced directly by Helvétius at all, he was active in getting utilitarianism established as the principle that has subsequently motivated the designers of fair taxation schemes for at least a hundred years.

Recall that Helvétius argued that there is no need to invoke what Sidgwick called ethical hedonism as a system of personal morality in order to support utilitarianism as an instrument of public policy. The problem of why a person should seek to maximize the sum of all utilities instead of their own utility then disappears. One can support a utilitarian government that enforces utilitarian policies without any need to abandon the psychological hedonism that implies that people will look after their own personal interests.

The case of taxation makes the point particularly well. Nobody likes paying their taxes, but we pay what we cannot avoid paying because we must. When voting for a new government that will enforce their taxation policy, some of us even take into account the insurance argument for utilitarianism that originated with Edgeworth.

Optimal income tax. Edgeworth's 1897 contribution was entirely theoretical. He asked what policy on income tax would be employed by a utilitarian government. Given various simplifying assumptions—notably decreasing marginal utility—he came to the extreme conclusion that taxation should neutralize all differences in income. Such an egalitarian conclusion would require progressive tax rates that put to shame those of even the most socialist of governments!

But no government has gone that far, partly because some of the issues left out of Edgeworth's model actually matter a lot. In particular, as William Vickrey pointed out some fifty years later, an equalizing tax schedule would play havoc with the incentives that encourage people to work harder. But a further half century passed before James Mirrlees finally produced a scheme for optimal utilitarian taxation that addresses enough of the outstanding issues to be generally regarded as a solving the various problems that Edgeworth left hanging in the air. The 1996 Nobel prize for economics was awarded to Vickrey and Mirrlees for this work.

12.3 Edgeworth's Life

Francis Edgeworth (1845–1926) was born to a freewheeling Irish family who had an estate in Edgeworthstown, County Longford. His father was on his way to study in Germany when he abandoned the trip to elope with a Catalan woman after meeting her on the steps of the British Museum. She christened the baby Edgeworth, Ysidro Francis, but he preferred to be called Francis Ysidro.

He had so many siblings and cousins that it must have been hard to keep track of them all, but he was eventually the only male left in line to inherit the family estate. It was probably no great source of income by the time he inherited, but Edgeworth had very little interest in what could be bought with money, and lived the spartan life of a devoted bachelor scholar until his death.

Edgeworth was educated at home by various tutors until it was time to study classics at Trinity College Dublin, from where he moved on to study ancient and modern languages at Balliol College, Oxford. He qualified as a barrister in London in 1877 but did not practice. With such a background, it is remarkable that he should have made his reputation through a series of original works in economics and statistics, but all the mathematical expertise he needed for this purpose was the product of private study without any help from anyone. He was appointed to a Chair of Economics at King's College London in 1888, and then to the Drummond Chair of Political Economy at Oxford in 1891. For 35 years, he edited the *Economic Journal*. which was the leading journal for economics in those days.

He is remembered nowadays for a whole series of ideas, of which only the highlights will be mentioned. In economics, the Edgeworth box is a standard tool in teaching the properties of equilibria in perfectly competitive markets.[3] The Bertrand-Edgeworth model of imperfect competition continues to be quoted in legal disputes over regulatory infractions. He is equally famous in statistics—in particular

---

[3] I am told that the Edgeworth box should really be attributed to Pareto, but that Pareto efficiency was really first formulated by Edgeworth.

for the concept of an Edgeworth series.

However, his fame as a utilitarian pioneer rests on the books *New and Old Methods of Ethics*—whose title deliberately echoes Sidgwick's *Methods of Ethics*—and the delightfully named *Mathematical Psychics*. It is unfortunate that Edgeworth's exotic writing style blunted the impact of these two books. He wrote as though the reader was as much of a polymath as the author. He thought nothing of long sentences that begin with the differential calculus, and end with an untranslated tag in classical Greek summarizing the sentence's conclusions.

The milieu that shaped Edgeworth's contributions to utilitarianism has been covered in the previous three chapters. He commented freely on the works of John Stuart Mill and of Henry Sidgwick, although when it came to political economy, he sided with Alfred Marshall. But the big influence on him was William Jevons. When not living in his rooms in Oxford, Edgeworth occupied a tiny apartment in London's Hampstead—in those days an airy suburb looking down on the smoky center of the British Empire. Jevons was a neighbor. They used to take long walks together on Hampstead Heath, as a consequence of which Edgeworth was supposedly converted to the study of economics. What a pity no transcripts of these conversations are available!

Chapter 13
Hare

13.1 Utilitarianism in Retreat

Richard Hare shares with John Harsanyi the misfortune of being an advocate of utilitarianism at a time when it was regarded as a quaint survival from the Victorian era. This attitude is evident in an influential collection of essays called *Utilitarianism and Beyond*,[1] in which Hare and Harsanyi were allowed space to put their supposedly outdated take on why utilitarianism should still be taken seriously, but the other essays are all about various more fashionable alternatives.

The chapter on Jevons tells how the Chicago School succeeded in discrediting utilitarianism among economists in the 1930s, but Hare would have been immune to propaganda from such a source. His problem lay in seeking to reconcile his utilitarianism with the kind of linguistic philosophy that held his Oxford colleagues in thrall in the 1950s. For example, moral naturalism supposedly consists of the hopeless task of finding naturalistic definitions of the words we use when talking about morality—as though our ancestors buried the secrets of how morality works in the language that evolved alongside them. Its guru was John Austin, the title of whose book *How to Do Things with Words* gives the general idea.

Moral Thinking. Richard Hare is of particular interest for us because his 1981 book *Moral Thinking*—in which he brought up to date the views expressed in his 1951 *Language of Morals* and his 1965 *Freedom and Reason*—reveals him to be a termite who was deeply interested, not just in the problems that Jeremy Bentham left unsolved in his unfinished agenda, but in how they are to be squared with both the Oxford philosophy of language, and the metaphysics of Immanuel Kant. Even the moral emotivism deriving ultimately from the Vienna Circle found its way

---

[1] Edited by Amartya Sen and Bernard Williams. Bernard Williams was one of several of Hare's students who went on to become leading philosophers in their own right, but abandoned Hare's utilitarianism. Peter Singer is an exception. He eventually made a bigger splash in the philosophical world than his fellow students by applying his mentor's utilitarian convictions to controversial areas like animal rights and global poverty. I am grateful to Singer for his help in correcting several of my mistakes, but he should by no means be taken as endorsing everything I say.

into his work. If he had not been ensnared in this way by the intellectual fashions that held sway in his time, perhaps he would be numbered today among the great utilitarian philosophers like Bentham and Mill.

13.2 Preference Utilitarianism

Hare is insistent that he favors preference utilitarianism over hedonic utilitarianism. He illustrates the difference by imagining a machine that stimulates the pleasure centers of the brain. Such a machine has actually been tried out on rats in recent years. They prefer pressing a lever that operates an electrode suitably located in their brains to everything else, including food and sex. In Hare's view, a human hedonist is likely to do the same, but someone who thinks hard about morality will choose not to use the machine. In any case, hedonic utilitarianism goes wrong in arguing that seeking pleasure or happiness should be taken to be the ultimate aim of a human being. It should be based on whatever a person's preferences actually are.

The Chicago School—and economists in general—would approve of this judgement. They hold that it is not for do-gooders to tell us what we ought to want. We can decide that for ourselves.

But suppose what people want is just to be happy, as argued by John Stuart Mill in his *Utilitarianism*. It is true that a do-gooder like Mill found it necessary to stretch the definition of what makes people happy to fit this claim, but with a more natural understanding of happiness, someone who seeks no more than to be happy would have hedonistic preferences, for whom preference utilitarianism and hedonic utilitarianism would be the same thing—a possibility we return to in the chapter on Harsanyi.

It follows that Hare and other philosophers to this day do not regard pleasure or happiness as a purely subjective phenomenon. They hang on to the Benthamite line that happiness is an objective phenomenon that could in principle be measured on a meter. The behavior of rats whose pleasure centers are artificially tickled certainly provides evidence that this much-mocked hypothesis is not so crazy after all. On the other hand, the modern theory of revealed preference mentioned in the chapter on Hume would assign these same rats an overwhelming preference for happiness.

13.3 Prescriptivity

I think it unlikely that Hare ever considered seriously the possibility that morality is a natural phenomenon in the style of David Hume. He would have found the moral relativism to which this view of the world leads abhorrent, but he was too intellectually honest to pretend to believe that moral relativism is the same as moral subjectivism, according to which we all absurdly make up our own personal morality for ourselves. For Hare, the same morality applies universally to all rational entities, as argued by Immanuel Kant.

13.3. PRESCRIPTIVITY

To the extent that his methodology is borrowed from Kant, Hare was a rationalist rather than an empiricist. He was therefore unable to follow the line of Helvétius when explaining why we are obliged to follow utilitarian imperatives when they conflict with our personal preferences. As with Kant's categorical imperative, such imperatives must be enforced by some agency within ourselves, rather than being attributed to a benign government seeking popular support. As Kant put it, it is rational to obey the laws you make for yourself.[2]

However, unlike Kant and followers like Harsanyi, he did not think it adequate simply to assume that we have an internal enforcement agency of the kind that the German idealists called the Will, and Harsanyi called Moral Commitment. Such skyhooks were not capable of satisfying a termite like Hare. In the manner natural to the place and time in which he found himself, he looked for an explanation in the way we use words when talking about moral issues

What does ought mean? People often say that we ought to do something but do something else instead. Hare argues that intuitive moralists—whom he calls proles—may use language in this way, but critical thinkers—whom he calls archangels—will work harder at teasing out the true meaning of ought. For example, proles will be satisfied with some version of rule utilitarianism, but archangels will see that only act utilitarianism makes proper sense.

I have to admit that I do not understand how Hare reconciles this way of thinking with his denial of Sidgwick's view that there is an inherent ambiguity in how we reason about practical matters. Hare seems to think that the intuitive reasoning of proles somehow sets the scene for the critical analysis of archangels, and so there is no need to choose between them. I see that we do not always have the time to think critically about moral events—like whether to save Archbishop Fénelon or your mother from a fire—and so must sometimes act as prompted by our untutored intuition, but a termite like Hare must surely have better reasons than this.

In any case, Hare argues that the meaning of the word *ought* when critically examined entails that someone cannot honestly say "I ought to do something" without making an irrevocable commitment to do that something should the occasion arise. That is to say, the word *ought* is unconditionally prescriptive when used sincerely.

Contemporary critics argued that this prescriptive definition of the word *ought* amounts to a denial that akrasia—weakness of the will—is a real phenomenon. That is to say, they doubted the existence of an internal skyhook called the Will that is able to suppress our future urges to deviate from a moral decision made in the past. Even metaphysically minded folk must have similar doubts that we can rely on the Will of our fellow human beings to behave morally when temptation is near. So it cannot be said that Hare's proposed solution of the enforcement problem for utilitarianism carries much conviction.

---

[2] Or, more obscurely, "Man needs a master to break his will that he might be free." I think the master here is Kant's concept of a transcendental Will that overrides the weakness of our ordinary wills. It makes us free because adding the power of making irrevocable commitments to our intellectual repertoire expands our feasible set of behaviors.

13.4 Universalizability

Prescriptivity is the first plank of Hare's theory. Its second plank is universability—that the same moral principles apply to everyone everywhere, a view that he attributes to Kant. Kant certainly argues very forcefully that moral principles must be universal, but so does Jeremy Bentham when insisting that everybody should count for one, and nobody for more than one. Indeed the idea that morality should apply equally to everybody goes back at least two thousand years to Epicurus, although Hare would not have approved of Epicurus's relativism in continuing the observation that "what counts as fair is the same for everybody" by restricting this to whatever social contract may be in place in some particular society, but which need not be the same in a different society, or in the same society at different times in its history.

Golden rule? How is the universalizability criterion to be applied? At this point, Hare follows the ideal observer tradition mentioned in the chapter on Edgeworth, but he does not reference Edgeworth, and seems unaware of his insurance argument. As with most other moral philosophers, his lack of any mathematical expertise would have made Edgeworth incomprehensible. Hare attributes his own take on the ideal observer approach to Clarence (C. I.) Lewis who was perhaps the leading American philosopher in the years before the Second World War.

Hare's ideal observer is called an Archangel to signal that he represents the reasoning to which all sufficiently critical thinkers will supposedly be led by thinking carefully enough. This reasoning tells us what we ought to do. Hare reiterates his view that the word *ought* should be interpreted as being prescriptive, then explains why we would act as utilitarians if we were convinced by the Archangel's arguments.

The impartiality of Hare's critical thinker is embodied in the Golden Rule recognized by intuitive thinkers of all cultures and religions down the ages. However, Hare's insistence that everything be referred back to the actual preferences of the citizens of the society to which his Archangel's reasoning is to be applied, leads him to adopt a more sophisticated interpretation of the Golden Rule than is usual.

He takes the line that it is not enough that I should do as I would be done by, because the person I plan to do something for may have different preferences from mine. The Archangel must therefore put himself in the shoes of each of the citizens of his society to see things from his or her point of view. In particular, he must accept that if he were occupying Alice's shoes, he would have her preferences rather than his own. For example, he might prefer coffee to tea, but if Alice prefers tea to coffee, he would not have succeeded in empathizing with her successfully if he proceeds as though he would still like coffee better than tea if he were her.

It is difficult at this stage to separate Hare's thinking from Harsanyi's on this issue because they discussed these matters at length. Who learned what from whom? My own guess is that they probably arrived at the need to adopt a sophisticated version of the Golden Rule independently. Since this turns out to be the philosophical key to Harsanyi's solution of the problem of interpersonal comparison of utility that Bentham left hanging in the air, it is therefore possible that Hare might have anticipated Harsanyi in coming up with a solution if he had only a little mathematical knowledge.

As things stand, Hare deserves to be congratulated in understanding that the problem of interpersonal comparison cannot be be brushed aside as a tiresome technical issue, as was the current philosophical practice in his time. But If we do not understand how to compare Alice and Bob's utility, what is the point of saying that we ought to maximize the sum of their utilities?

Hare advanced matters to the stage where he saw the need to invoke the idea of David Hume and Adam Smith that empathetic preferences are relevant to interpersonal comparison. This was a major step forward, but Hare was unable to take this insight beyond expressing philosophical generalities about its implications. When we come to discuss how Harsanyi—who was no great shakes as a mathematician either—managed to go further, we ought therefore to remind ourselves that Richard Hare might have been there first if he had not been so heavily influenced by the philosophical fashions of his time.

13.5 Hare's Life

Richard Hare (1919–2002) was born to well-off parents, but was orphaned at an early age, and cared for by a succession of relatives and guardians until he was old to be sent off to school. He enjoyed an elite education, culminating in Oxford's Balliol College, where he studied classics.

When war broke out, he put aside his pacifist convictions to join the army, but was taken prisoner at the fall of Singapore to the Japanese in 1942. He must have suffered terribly alongside the other prisoners-of-war who were used as slave labor on the death railway through Thailand, but was reluctant to speak about his experiences in later years, beyond observing that he sought to create a system that would serve as a guide to life even in the harshest conditions.

After the war, he was elected to a fellowship at Balliol College, after which he ascended through the Oxford academic hierarchy, eventually becoming the White Professor of Moral Philosophy in 1966.

He married in 1947, and was blessed with three children, one of whom grew up to be another philosopher. He chose to live an austere life, but he was more than a cloistered scholar. He took an almost parental interest in his students, and wrote extensively on how ethical thinking should inform matters of public concern, for which efforts he is regarded as one of the founders of the discipline of applied ethics.

Rather than retire in 1983, he moved to a research position at the University of Florida at Gainesville. He returned to England in 1994, where he died after a series of strokes in 2002.

He left behind a "A Philosophical Autobiography" to be published after his death. It says more about him than is possible for any short biography—although the account of his life in Stanford's online Philosophical Encyclopedia is very good. The autobiography accepts that his high hopes for his philosophical ideas were not to be realiized—that "hard-working philosophical worms" would nibble away at his system to reveal that his achievements were mere illusion. As things turned out, the worms found Harsanyi a more tempting target.

Chapter 14
Rawls

14.1 Rawls a Utilitarian?

The most successful of the efforts in the 1950s to move beyond utilitarianism was John Rawls' novel defense of egalitarianism. His 1971 *Theory of Justice* continues to be regarded as the leading work of moral philosophy of the last century.

The *Theory of Justice* was explicitly written to provide a reasoned alternative to utilitarianism, so why is Rawls included in a book about utilitarians? This chapter argues that Rawls's foundational assumptions should actually have led him to a utilitarian conclusion. This may seem a bold claim, but Richard Hare was even bolder in suggesting that Immanuel Kant should really be regarded as a utilitarian in spite of his deontological rhetoric.

The original position. In consulting his moral intuition in the naturalistic style advocated by Hutcheson, Rawls found it unacceptable that utilitarianism should sometimes call for minorities to be sacrificed to enhance the welfare of the majority.[1] He therefore wrote the *Theory of Justice* to argue that foundations for egalitarianism can be found that are no less convincing than the arguments for utilitarianism, which otherwise continued to have no serious rival. In doing so, Rawls invented a device he called the *original position* for making fairness judgements that frames the abstract insurance argument of Edgeworth in a manner that chimes sufficiently well with our shared moral intuitions that people hearing of it for the first time often express delight in its capturing the essence of how our everyday fairness norms work in practice.

Natural Duty? The fact that a close analysis of Rawls' analysis of rational behavior in the original position should arguably have made him a utilitarian rather than an egalitarian does not necessarily imply that his own egalitarian moral intuitions are misplaced. The chapter therefore closes with a brief review of my

---

[1] As in the story of the missionaries and the cannibals in the chapter on Bentham, or the story of the surgical transfer of eyes in the chapter on Helvétius.

own reinterpretation of Rawls' defense of egalitarianism in naturalistic terms that Hutcheson's religious convictions would have led him to reject in horror. In this reinterpretation, I attempt to explain how the original position might have evolved as a coordination device in primitive food-sharing arrangements.

Rawls' foundational skyhook of Natural Duty that supposedly enforces the hypothetical agreements reached in the original position then has to be abandoned, but it turns out that abandoning this skyhook is exactly what is needed to generate egalitarian conclusions rather than utilitarian conclusions.[2]

14.2 Reflective Equilibrium

Was Rawls a termite or a moth? He sounds like a termite when he echoes Sidgwick by writing: "We should strive for a kind or moral geometry with all the rigor that this name connotes." However, Rawls' notion of a reflective equilibrium denies the naive interpretation that there are self-evident moral axioms from which egalitarianism can be deduced by logical reasoning in the style of Euclid.

According to Rawls, a reflective equilibrium in moral science is reached in the same way that models are constructed in the physical sciences, where theories are sought that are consistent with the data observed. One does not begin with axioms—like the ancient notion that planets must move in perfect circles—and seek to reconcile the data with such preconceptions. Instead one takes the data as given, and seeks axioms that imply the data. However, in moral science, the physical data of science are replaced by the moral intuitions that Rawls echoed Hutcheson in believing are to be found inside our own heads. I suspect Rawls thought he was following Sidgwick in advocating this approach, and perhaps he was.

In any case, the question is not whether egalitarianism follows from self-evident moral axioms. The question is: What moral axioms need to be adopted to make egalitarianism a logical consequence? Rawls' answer is that we need to abandon the neoclassical orthodoxy that rationality requires maximizing expected utility in risky situations in favor of the maximin principle that one should always assume a worst-case scenario when deciding what to do.

John Harsanyi—the subject of the next chapter—invented the original position independently of Rawls at about the same time in the 1950s. He found that maximizing expected utility in the original position leads to utilitarianism. Who is right: Rawls or Harsanyi? This chapter offers an original analysis that comes down in favor of Harsanyi when some way of enforcing the hypothetical deals reached in the original position is available. It is argued that Rawls' cavalier attitude to rationality is so counter-intuitive as to outweigh any moral intuition that might point in the opposite direction.[3]

---

[2] As Rawls nearly convinces himself when writing the third part of his *Theory of Justice*, which addresses the "strains of commitment" that his Natural Duty skyhook must somehow withstand.

[3] I hope this new analysis is more convincing than Harsanyi's "Can the Maximin Principle Serve as a Basis for Morality: A Critique of John Rawls's Theory" *American Political Science Review* 69 (1975), (594–606), where he implicitly dismisses Rawls' attempts at finding foundations for egalitarianism as painfully amateurish. In particular, Harsanyi's brusque critique fails to appreciate

14.3 Original Position

Rawls describes the original position as an operationalization of Immanuel Kant's categorical imperative. I prefer to think of it as a refinement of the Golden Rule which accepts that Alice should not always do unto Bob as she would have Bob do unto her—because his tastes may not be the same as hers. Anthropologists report that some version of the Golden Rule is universal in human societies, and so it seems a relatively safe candidate for a shared moral intuition in the human species.

Veil of ignorance. When a fairness judgement is to be made using the original position, Alice and Bob imagine themselves behind a *veil of ignorance* that conceals their identities. Behind the veil of ignorance, Alice thinks that she has an equal chance of turning out to be either Alice or Bob, and the same goes for Bob. In this hypothetical state of ignorance, they imagine themselves bargaining about how to reach a compromise in whatever sharing problem they may face.

For this purpose, the bargainers need to be equipped with the empathetic preferences mentioned in the chapters on Hume and Hare that specify how someone in the original position compares ending up in Alice's shoes in one situation with ending up in Bob's shoes in another. The fact that people are able to express such empathetic preferences can be seen as supporting Rawls' contention that the original position is built into our shared moral intuitions. What other function do empathetic preferences serve other than as inputs to the device of the original position when used to resolve fairness questions?

Who gets what? What deal would be reached if Alice and Bob were to bargain behind the veil of ignorance? One conclusion follows immediately. Whatever compromise they reach will be Pareto efficient, which means that no deal is available that both would prefer. If Alice and Bob are rational, why would they agree on a wasteful inefficient deal when another deal is available in which they both get more?[4]

Which of the many Pareto efficient deals available to Alice and Bob in the original position will be chosen? The answer depends on how we model Alice and Bob as rational agents. Rawls' model of rationality behind the veil of ignorance leads to egalitarianism. Harsanyi's model leads to utilitarianism.

But the immediate point is why people uninterested in the issues that separate Rawls and Harsanyi are so ready to accord with the moral intuition that the agreement reached in the original position will be fair. The answer is the same

---

that Rawls's method of reflective equilibrium makes the axioms from which deductions are made open to revision if the theorems to which they lead are counter-intuitive.

[4]The Chicago School refer to the proposition that rational bargainers will not agree on a deal that is Pareto inefficient as the Coase Theorem, but the idea that it is irrational for two bargainers to settle on a deal that is inefficient when other deals are available that make both bargainers better off already appears in Edgeworth's 1881 *Mathematical Psychics*. It arises as part of his definition of the contract curve of deals available to two traders seeking to barter their endowments of different commodities. Which of the many Pareto efficient deals on the contract curve will be chosen? Edgeworth suggests resolving this problem on utilitarian principles.

as for Edgeworth's insurance argument. The distribution of advantage in whatever compromise Alice and Bob reach behind the veil of ignorance will seem determined as though by a lottery—and devil take the hindmost is an unattractive principle, if you yourself might end up with the lottery ticket that assigns you to the rear.

Social contracts. Rawls sees himself as part of the social contract tradition of Locke, Rousseau and Kant mentioned in the chapter on Hutcheson. So it is not enough for him to consider the problem faced by Alice and Bob in the original position. Rawls needs to imagine the whole of society in a town-hall meeting reminiscent of the conclaves of Grotius and Pufendorf, but located not in some mythical past, but behind Rawls' veil of ignorance. Rawls' *Theory of Justice* argues that such a meeting will then agree on two utopian principles of justice that liberal moths find very attractive:

1. Each person is to have an equal right to the most extensive basic liberty compatible with a similar liberty for others.
2. Social and economic inequalities are to be arranged so that they are both (a) to the greatest benefit of the least advantaged and (b) attached to offices and positions open to all under conditions of fair equality of opportunity.

Maximin in—maximin out. Rawls requires that his first principle of justice take absolute priority over the second. Only when the rights and liberties to which it refers have been secured are the distributional questions treated by the second principle to be considered.[5]

Rawls arrives at part (a) of the second principle—which he calls the difference principle—by proposing that rational agents in the original position will employ the maximin criterion rather than the maximization of expected utility.

Why equal outcomes? It is necessary to put aside for the moment the question of why the maximin criterion should be preferred to maximizing expected utility in the original position. The reason is that the late Derek Parfit has gained some traction with health gurus in promoting what he calls prioritarianism, in which improving the welfare of the worst-off class takes priority over everything else.

Parfit therefore advocates abandoning the egalitarian conclusions that Rawls favors. In fact, Parfit seeks to discredit egalitarianism—as he earlier sought to discredit utilitarianism—by reviving the story of an imaginary world in which living eyes can be surgically transferred from one person to another so that the blind can be made to see. He then makes fun of an invented version of egalitarianism in which equality is achieved by blinding everybody.[6] But such a spectacularly

---

[5] In his later *Political Liberalism*, Rawls responded to criticism of his *Theory of Justice* by restricting his claims to societies with a democratic tradition, in which his principles of justice are more easily defended.

[6] See Parfit's *Equality or Priority*, which is a lecture whose transcript can be googled. Parfit's attempt to discredit utilitarianism is described in the chapter on Hutcheson.

inefficient outcome is ruled out by the original position, which adjudicates only between Pareto-efficient outcomes.

It is a pity that Rawls' statement of his second principle of justice seems to endorse the inequalities that would remain after a prioritarian reform, as no such inequalities can survive when the original position is applied in situations when compromises are always available between any rival deals that might be on the table.[7] The mathematical requirement is that the set of possible deals available in the original position be convex.

In the examples that Rawls gives of unequal outcomes, the set of possible deals is very non-convex. His second principle of justice is stated in terms of the maximin criterion rather than equality so as not to exclude these unusual non-convex cases. Parfit was famously scathing about the very possibility that mathematics could ever be relevant to moral thinking, and so failed to understand this point. However, one does not need to be able to draw a diagram showing that the maximin criterion will assign equal outcomes to Alice and Bob when their feasible set is convex to see why people bargaining in the original position will normally be led to an egalitarian outcome.

In brief, there is no reason why the bargaining behind the veil of ignorance should stop when the lot of the least well-off class has been brought up to the level of the next class up. All that one succeeds in doing this way is to create a larger class of the least well-off, whose lot now has to be improved to bring them into line with the class above the new class of unfortunates. Continuing in this way leads inevitably to equality in normal circumstances.

14.4 Why Maximin?

I am not sure that Rawls was aware of the truly iconoclastic implications of his claim that the maximin criterion can be regarded as a viable alternative to the maximization of expected utility in rational decision theory. So it is perhaps worth drawing attention to the fact that the work of James Milnor makes it possible to identify exactly what has to be denied if the maximization of expected utility is replaced by the maximin criterion.

Alice is making decisions in a situation in which the consequences of her choice are uncertain. If she prefers action a to action b, Rudin's axiom says that she will also prefer action a to action b, even if there is some probability that something will happen that makes her choice of action irrelevant to what happens next. Milnor shows that it is precisely this axiom that needs to be denied if expected utility theory is to be replaced by the maximin criterion. But who would want to deny Rudin's axiom as a principle of rational choice?[8]

---

[7] The compromises might involve physical mixes of the rival outcomes, or if they cannot be mixed, making who gets what dependent on the fall of a dice, or the day of the week.

[8] Milnor is best known for his magnificent book *Differential Topology*. The work cited in the text is "Games against Nature" in *Decision Processes* edited by Thrall, Coombs and Davies, Wiley, New York, 1954. A simplified account appears in my book *Rational Decisions* (pp. 157–193). Milnor calls Rudin's axiom the condition of Column Linearity.

Milnor actually gives a whole bunch of axioms, and identifies which subsets from these axioms characterize various choice criteria in the symmetric case when Alice has no reason to think that any of the uncertain states of the world are more likely than any their fellows. The axioms that characterize expected utility theory and the maximin criterion are the same except in the case of Rudin's axiom, which has to be denied for the maximin criterion, and replaced by axioms that make assigning probabilities to the uncertainties that Alice faces an impossibility.[9]

If one wanted to defend Rawls' use of the maximin criterion in the original position in spite of its violation of Rudin's axiom, the best approach would therefore seem to be to redefine the circumstances of the original position so that the question of who will become whom after Alice and Bob emerge from behind the veil of ignorance is made so uncertain that assigning probabilities to the two possibilities ceases to be meaningful. There is even a school of economists who support the use of the maximin criterion in such circumstances.[10]

However, my guess is that Rawls would have been decidedly hostile to basing moral principles that may affect people's lives—especially in considering the ethics of public health care—on whether one adopts this or that axiom in abstract discussions of rational choice theory. He was interested in such matters only to the extent that they provide input when seeking to refine our moral intuitions.

14.5 Deducing Utilitarianism

In Milnor's analysis, Alice can be taken to seek to maximize her long-run average subjective happiness when evaluating the possible consequences of her actions. But Rawls finds the Benthamite notion of happiness as the excess of pleasure over pain too crude. So he replaces happiness by some aggregate of what he calls primary goods.[11] In Harsanyi's own very similar version of the original position, happiness is replaced by neoclassical utility.

With these assumptions about their aims, Alice and Bob are now imagined to bargain in the original position about how to share what is available when they emerge from behind the veil of ignorance. Both Rawls and Harsanyi dodge the problem of modeling how Alice and Bob bargain by making assumptions that render Alice and Bob identical in the original position.[12] So their bargaining reduces to agreeing on whatever sharing rule they jointly regard as optimal. If they are both

---

[9]Milnor's Column Duplication. axiom implies that Alice will take account only of the best and worst possible consequences of her actions. A little more is needed to get the maximin criterion.

[10]See, for example, Gilboa's "Maximin expected utility with non-unique priors" in the 2004 volume *Uncertainty in Economics: Essays in Honor of David Schmeidler's 65th Birthday*.

[11]Those relevant when applying the maximin criterion are income and wealth, the powers and prerogatives of office, and the social basis of self-respect.

[12]An argument relying on the original position is then reduced simply to retelling Edgeworth's insurance story with the identical Alice and Bob substituting for an Ideal Observer. This was in fact how Harsanyi framed his original defense of utilitarianism, but people find the story told in terms of the original position much more convincing. I suspect this is because the original position captures the basic structure of the fairness norms we use in ordinary life in resolving everyday coordination problems like determining whose turn it is to wash the dishes tonight.

modeled as maximizers of long-run average utility (however conceived), the outcome will therefore be the average of the utilities that each will receive after the veil of ignorance is lifted. The argument is totally trivial, but the conclusion is precisely what utilitarianism recommends.

Maximizing average utility is the same as maximizing the sum of utilities in a population of fixed size, but the preceding argument can be deployed even when the size of the population is allowed to vary. Parfit's rejection of the repugnant implications of utilitarianism then falls to the ground, since the sum of utilities in a society in which nearly everybody is living a barely tolerable life may indeed be large, but its average utility will be small. Parfit responds to this standard response to his repugnant story by observing that we could improve the average utility of a society by eliminating everybody but its happiest citizen. But the happiest person is unlikely to remain happy if entirely alone! Nor would the utility of a citizen in a repugnant society remain constant as more and more people were added. It is because it would decline that we think of such a society as repugnant. However, I prefer to defend utilitarianism only in the case of fixed population size, rather then address the issue of how population size is likely to effect individual happiness.

14.6 Bentham's Unfinished Agenda

What progress does introducing the original position bring in addressing Bentham's unfinished agenda? The questions he left unanswered are listed again below.

How is utility measured? Unless Rawls' notion of primary goods can be operationalized somehow, there is no progress here. However, this subject is taken up in the next chapter on Harsanyi, where his use of neoclassical expected utility can be defended as a necessary requirement if Alice and Bob are sufficiently rational as to make decisions in a consistent manner.

How are the utilities of different people to be compared? One can separate this question into two, although I do not believe Bentham himself ever raised the second question. How is Alice's utility to be compared with Bob's? Why should everybody agree on how this comparison is to be made?

Rawls evades both questions. On the second question, he simply observes that real people actually do share their attitudes to making interpersonal comparisons to a large degree. One may agree with Rawls that societies do in fact maintain a broad consensus on how comparisons should be made within a particular context, but how is this consensus achieved? How does the consensus vary between contexts?

Why add the utilities of different people? The device of the original position forces people to proceed as though they are equally likely to find themselves in the shoes of any of their fellow citizens when they emerge from behind the veil of ignorance. If they are long-run maximizers of average utility, they will therefore behave as classical utilitarians because maximizing average utility is the same as maximizing the sum of utilities when the size of the population is fixed.

Why should I maximize the sum of utilities rather than my own? More generally, why do Alice and Bob honor the hypothetical deal supposedly reached in the original position?

Rawls' answer is that they have a Natural Duty to do so. To press the point home, he observes that a slave-holding society would not be agreed in the original position, but if it were, the Natural Duty of those designated as slaves would be to acquiesce in their enslavement. Harsanyi's answer simply substitutes the words Moral Commitment for Natural Duty. Helvétius would answer that inventing such skyhooks is unnecessary. Governments take care of enforcement. The original position is merely a conventional device that allows Alice and Bob to coordinate their efforts in promoting a fair form of government.

14.7 Gentleman and Scholar

I was lucky enough to have the opportunity to discuss my own project to naturalize Rawls' theory of justice with Rawls himself. People describe him as being of a retiring nature, and plagued with a stutter. He was certainly almost absurdly modest, but I found his stutter hardly noticeable. Although he was a lifelong follower of Kant, he later wrote me a long letter—handwritten in beautiful copperplate—in which he encouraged me in my project. I was left feeling that if everybody were like Rawls, there would be no need for moral philosophy at all.

John Rawls (1921–2002) ended up as a much-loved philosophy professor at Harvard, but his early life was no bourgeois idyll. He was deeply affected by the death of two of his brothers after they contracted illnesses from him. His later service in the Second World War as an enlisted man in the appalling trench war during the retaking of the Philippines was traumatic. He had intended to become a priest after the war, but seeing the aftermath of the nuclear bombing of Nagasaki and Hiroshima while serving during the later occupation of Japan made him into an atheist.

I was to meet Rawls again at a 1996 conference in Caen, France, where he and Harsanyi were to be awarded honorary doctorates, but he was unable to attend after the first of a series of heart attacks that kept him in his bed most of the time until his death in 2002.

14.8 Naturalizing Rawls

In this section, I have yielded to the temptation to say something about my own attempt to naturalize Rawls' foundations for egalitarianism. The details are to be found in my *Natural Justice*, which is a non-mathematical summary of my much longer *Game Theory and the Social Contract*.

Sharing food. Since I am the kind of termite who builds towers of metaphorical mud and saliva that have no truck with metaphysical skyhooks at all, my foundations offer an explanation of how Rawls' device of the original position might have evolved as an equilibrium selection device when our ancestors were confronted with coordination games with many equilibria. The sharing of food is the most obvious example. Alice and Bob can both gain by insuring themselves against hunger by agreeing to share food, but who is to get how much when a carcase is to be divided?

Such food-sharing understandings are commonplace in the animal kingdom, but the arrangements amongst our prehuman ancestors cannot originally have been utilitarian because of the problem of enforcement. Originally, any deals that evolved must have been self-enforcing.[13] It is only later that the coalition of all the members of a hunter-gatherer community could have provided the enforcement that Hevétius attributes to a government. I speculate that the device of the original position was imprinted in our genes at an earlier stage, which is why Rawls and his followers (including me) have moral intuitions that favor egalitarianism so strongly.

Evolutionary ethics is nonsense? The late Bernard Williams used to make fun of my attempts at a termite's tower as being no less of a just-so story than the metaphysical skyhooks of the moths.[14] It is true that little objective data can be marshalled in support of my evolutionary story, since our ancestral social contracts left no fossils to be dug up. But the point of attempting to find evolutionary foundations for the concepts of fairness we find lodged as moral intuitions in our heads is not to come up with a model that mimics our actual evolutionary history, but to demonstrate that such a model is not an absurd impossibility.

Whole books like Paul Farber's *Temptations of Evolutionary Ethics* have been written denouncing the very idea that evolution—red in tooth and claw—could possibly be relevant to human ethics. But their arguments take for granted the very propositions they supposedly prove. For example, when Farber quotes the philosopher Theodore de Laguna as saying: "It has been demonstrated again and again that the Darwinian theory will lie down peacefully with almost any variety of ethical faith", he fails to consider that if all varieties of ethical faith do actually have evolutionary origins, then of course they will all be consistent with having evolutionary origins. Only someone whose mind is closed to the possibility that different societies might have different moralities could make such a mistake. And it is important to my theory that the standard of interpersonal comparison should be seen as the product of cultural evolution (rather than biological evolution), and hence dependent on the social context in which it evolved.

Deep structure of fairness norms. My *Natural Justice* argues that fairness norms are like language in that they all share a genetically determined deep structure, but differ from one society to another in their details, which are determined by

---

[13]Game theorists express Hume's idea that a convention must be self-enforcing by saying that it needs to coordinate behavior on a Nash equilibrium of whatever game is being played. It is important that the game being played is understood to be a repeated game with an indefinite horizon. The restriction of viable outcomes to Nash equilibria need then involve no loss of efficiency when the players have no secrets from each other.

[14]Bernard Williams (1929–2003) was a student of Richard Hare who became a distinguished moral philosopher in his own right. He was as dismissive of followers of Kant as he was of followers of Darwin like myself.

cultural evolution. Just as the French say *pain* where the English say *bread*, so one society will make interpersonal comparisons differently from another. David Hume would express this point by saying that the standard of comparison in a society is just a matter of convention.

For example, it was conventional in late Victorian times to regard women as intrinsically inferior to men. But the operant convention has changed so much since that time that we now find it distasteful when intellectual heroes of the past like Jevons and Edgeworth casually take for granted the superiority of men.

My model of the genetic origins of the original position as representing the deep structure of fairness norms mimics Edgeworth's insurance argument in tracing its origins to our ancestors finding ways to insure themselves against hunger by sharing food. To use the original position in real life, people need to be equipped with the empathetic preferences mentioned in the chapters on Hume and Hare, and discussed further in the coming chapter on Harsanyi. Such empathetic preferences determine how Alice's welfare is to be compared with Bob's. They are viewed as conventional constructs shaped by cultural evolution, whose study requires solving the bargaining problem that Alice and Bob face behind the veil of ignorance when they have different empathetic preferences. As these empathetic preferences evolve over time in my evolutionary model, they tend to coalesce, so that everybody will end up holding the same empathetic preferences—as Rawls claims to be true in practice.

Whether the fairness norms that are generated by this combination of biological and cultural evolution end up with a utilitarian or an egalitarian structure depends on the degree of available enforcement. It is for this reason that I think we find progressive income tax fair when enforced by a utilitarian government in the style advocated by Helvétius, but are more likely to regard egalitarian norms as fair in ordinary life.

Chapter 15
Harsanyi

15.1 Crying in the Wilderness?

John Harsanyi won the 1994 Nobel Prize in Economics for his Bayesian solution to the problem of incomplete information in game theory. One would have thought that this achievement alone would have been enough to gain the respect of the philosophical community, but Harsanyi is largely ignored by orthodox philosophers, in spite of his providing coherent answers to the utilitarian questions left hanging in the air by Jeremy Bentham.[1]

This neglect may perhaps be because Harsanyi couched his ideas in (not very deep) mathematical terms, or more likely, because the philosophy profession since the time of John Stuart Mill has shown little or no interest in tackling Bentham's unfinished agenda. The general view seems to have been that Mill's *Utilitarianism* had provided the answers already, although we have seen that Mill offered nothing that a termite would regard as an answer at all.

Original position. The chapter on Rawls tells the story of how Harsanyi independently invented the original position at about the same time as Rawls. Instead of following Rawls in defending egalitarianism by feeding the maximin criterion for individuals into the original position to get the maximin criterion for society out, he defended utilitarianism by feeding the maximization of average individual utility into the original position to get the maximization of average social utility out. Both Rawls' and Harsanyi's formal analyses are as trivial as this assessment makes them sound, but Harsanyi's defense of his assumptions using the neoclassical concept of utility amounts to offering answers to all the questions on what we have been calling Bentham's unfinished agenda that Bentham actually asked himself.

So this chapter begins by describing the invention of the neoclassical concept of utility by John von Neumann and Oskar Morgenstern in their 1944 groundbreaking *Theory of Games and Economic Behavior* that decision theorists usually refer to as von Neumann and Morgenstern utility. But before describing their theory, I think

---

[1] Alan Gibbard's Tanner lectures are a notable exception, as is John Broome's *Weighing Goods*.

it important to absolve Harsanyi of the unjustified complaint that his use of the theory denies him the right to be regarded as a utilitarian in direct succession to all the other utilitarians reviewed in this book.

Neoclassical utility and happiness. The activities of the Chicago School in the 1930s have set in stone the idea that neoclassical economists favor a world of rampant selfishness. Those who hold fast to this prejudice similarly reject out of hand the idea that neoclassical utility could possibly have any role in a discussion of human morality. The fact that the neoclassical theory of utility says that Alice maximizes her own expected utility is taken to confirm that she is assumed to care only about herself. But nothing in the theory implies that Alice does not have sympathetic preferences that take account of the welfare of others. Even St Francis of Assisi would serve as a model for maximizing expected neoclassical utility if he went about caring for others in a consistent way. Nor does Harsanyi's use of neoclassical utility necessarily conflict with regarding utility as an idealization of how ordinary people usually think about happiness.

Philosophers are free to define hedonic utilitarianism as requiring some objective measure of happiness that would allow do-gooders like Mill to tell us that they know what is good for us better than we know ourselves, but preference utilitarians like Harsanyi or Hare are equally free to follow Aristotle in regarding happiness as a subjective phenomenon, so that people can answer back when do-gooders seek to change their lives in ways that make them feel unhappy.

Amartya Sen. The authority of the Nobel laureate Amartya Sen[2] therefore needs to be discounted when he unthinkingly disputes Harsanyi's claim to be a utilitarian because Harsanyi is a preference utilitarian. It is, in fact, entirely obvious that people who consistently identify their own welfare with their long-run average happiness—as traditional utilitarians typically take for granted—will necessarily satisfy the consistency requirements of the neoclassical theory, with utility equal to happiness. The same goes for biological fitness. An animal that consistently behaves as though maximizing its long-run average fitness—as evolutionary biologists usually assume—will also satisfy the neoclassical theory, but with utility equal to fitness.

When Harsanyi borrows the mathematical techniques of neoclassical utility theory, he is therefore not stepping outside the traditional utilitarian approach, he is merely widening its scope. In particular, his approach allows a discussion of the foundations of utilitarianism to proceed independently of how happiness is defined, provided that the definition is applied consistently, and the kind of happiness defined is indeed what people actually want.

---

[2] Amartya Sen won the 1996 Nobel prize for economics largely for persuading economists that ethics matters. The paper where he denies that Harsanyi is a utilitarian is "Welfare economics and Rawlsian axiomatics" *Theory and Decision* 7 (1976), 243–262. His own paternalistic attempt to step beyond utilitarianism by offering an objective definition of what is good for people in terms of what new opportunities are made available to them—their capabilities—is very popular among developmental economists.

15.2 Neoclassical Cardinal Utility

The official foundations of neoclassical economics do not argue that people choose coffee over tea because their utility for coffee exceeds their utility for tea. It is not even argued that coffee is chosen over tea because coffee is preferred to tea. The theory of revealed preference introduced in the chapter on Hume begins with the actual choices people make. It says that if people choose consistently, then they will behave *as though* they are maximizing the expected value of an abstract something that we choose to call utility. It therefore abandons any attempt at a psychological explanation of what causes human choice behavior. If Alice's choice behavior is consistent for whatever reason, neoclassical economics merely observes that Alice can be modeled as a maximizer of expected utility.[3]

What is utility? This laid-back neoclassical attitude is very helpful for someone seeking foundations for utilitarianism. We no longer have to follow Mill in offering specious reasons to explain why some invented concept of happiness is what people really want. We only have to ask whether their choice behavior is consistent. If so, they can be modeled as maximizing the expected value of something. Whatever this something may be, we call it utility. If it coincides with a correlate of whatever is being called happiness, then well and good. If it coincides with an aggregate of Rawls' primary goods, even better. But utilitarians can join economists in leaving this question to psychologists. All that is needed to make sense of utility is that the citizens of a society make their individual choices in a consistent manner.[4]

How is utility measured? The chapter on Jevons tells the story of the 1930s jeremiads of Lionel Robbins against the very idea that cardinal utility could make sense. It was against this backdrop that Oskar Morgenstern turned up one afternoon in the 1940s at von Neumann's Princeton house to argue that they needed a better explanation of the payoffs in the games they were writing their famous book about. Von Neumann then sat right down, and wrote an axiomatic theory refuting Robbins' philosophical position on the spot.

Von Neumann's theory uses Alice's attitudes to risk to answer the question of how cardinal utility is to be measured—which is just what we need when applying Edgeworth's insurance argument for utilitarianism, whether offered straight, or in terms of Rawls' original position. The theory specifies consistency requirements that apply in a world whose uncertain prospects can be assigned objective probabilities, so expanding the original neoclassical theory of utility maximization in deterministic worlds to the maximization of *expected* utility in risky worlds.

---

[3] This approach has its origins in Paul Samuelson's 1940s theory of revealed preference in markets, which as currently generalized, would better be described as a theory of attributed preference and belief. My book *Rational Decisions* is one of many that give the mathematical details.

[4] Do real people behave consistently? The evidence from behavioral experiments is not very encouraging. To follow the neoclassical line pursued here is therefore at best a temporary expedient until we have better models of actual human behavior.

Analogy with temperature. The theory of von Neumann and Morgenstern is entirely explicit about how utility is to be measured. It is to be thought of like a temperature scale on which we are free to choose the zero and the unit, but after that everything is determined by Alice's choices.

Let us imagine that Alice first sets the zero and the unit on her utility scale to mimic how we set the zero and unit on a Celsius thermometer. Alice first needs to choose a very bad outcome—say that she is fired—to correspond to the freezing point of water. She then needs to choose a very good outcome—say that she inherits a fortune—to correspond to the boiling point of water. She can then assign 0 utils to being fired, and 100 utils to inheriting a fortune. How does she then assign utils to an intermediate outcome—say that she gets a raise of five dollars an hour in her current job?

The answer is that she compares such an intermediate outcome to a lottery in which she inherits a fortune some percentage of the time, and gets fired from her job the rest of the time. She adjusts the percentage of the time she gets the better of these two outcomes until she is indifferent between choosing the intermediate outcome and choosing the adjusted lottery. Perhaps this indifference point occurs when the percentage of the time in which she inherits a fortune in the lottery is 15%. If so, she should then assign 15 utils to getting a raise in her current job.

In the preceding story, Alice could have chosen to mimic how we set the zero and unit on a Fahrenheit thermometer. She would then have assigned 32 utils to her very bad outcome, and 212 utils to her very good outcome. We can then go back and forward between her two utility scales as we go back and forward between the Celsius and Fahrenheit scales using the formula $5(f - 32) = 9c$. The 15 utils she assigned to getting a raise on her old scale then become 59 utils on her new scale.

This is all the mathematics anyone needs to know to understand Harsanyi's solution to the problem of interpersonal comparison. The important thing is that 9 degrees Fahrenheit are equivalent to 5 degrees Celsius. For utilitarian applications, we can forget about where the zero goes on the two scales because adding constants to everybody's utility simply results in a bigger constant being added to a utilitarian sum, which does not make any difference when we work out what maximizes it.

Interpersonal comparison impossible? This discussion of alternative scales provides a good opportunity to make the important point that nothing in the theory of von Neumann and Morgenstern allows us to compare Alice's and Bob's utils. To do so without introducing some basis for making the comparison would be like deciding that it is warmer in the kitchen than the lounge because the kitchen thermometer has a higher reading than the lounge thermometer, when it could easily be the case that one thermometer is Celsius and the other Fahrenheit.

There may still be followers of Robbins who think this last point about interpersonal comparison implies that interpersonal comparison is an absurd impossibility, and therefore that fairness is a meaningless concept. But all that is implied by the fact that von Neumann and Morgenstern's assumptions do not justify making interpersonal comparisons is that additional assumptions are necessary. As we shall see, Harsanyi's addition was to apply the von Neumann and Morgenstern theory to the empathetic preferences first mentioned in the chapter on Hume.

Cardinality in question? While on the subject of the cardinality of von Neumann and Morgenstern utility functions, an aside is necessary on Amartya Sen's continuation of his claim that Harsanyi is not entitled to call himself a utilitarian. Worse still, Harsanyi's supposedly utilitarian welfare function is not even cardinal.

This complaint succeeds in being simultaneously untrue and irrelevant. It is true that the *expected value* of a von Neumann and Morgenstern utility function is not cardinal—any strictly increasing transformation of the expected value of a von Neumann and Morgenstern utility function will serve equally well to describe a person's preferences over lotteries, but so what? It is the cardinality of the von Neumann and Morgenstern function *itself* that people are talking about when they say that von Neumann and Morgenstern utility is cardinal.

In any case, what does it matter whether the welfare function Harsanyi constructs is cardinal or not? What matters is whether the utility functions of the individual citizens are cardinal, so that they can be compared, weighted, and summed.[5]

How is it possible that such a silly complaint should have formed the basis of extended philosophical debate? I guess what the critics who nibble at Harsanyi's arguments are really complaining about is utilitarianism itself. They would be more honest to say so outright, rather than kicking up dust by inventing specious technical reasons to discredit Harsanyi's defense of utilitarianism.

15.3 Two Defenses of Utilitarianism

Harsanyi offers two defenses of utilitarianism, the first of which is the same as Richard Hare's, except that Harsanyi's ideal observer accepts the logic of Edgeworth's insurance argument, so that all Harsanyi needs to borrow directly from the Golden Rule is that everybody should be treated equally.[6] Harsanyi also shares Hare's view that people ought to honor utilitarian principles even when they conflict with their personal preferences, but rather than attempt to justify proceeding in this way by analyzing the meaning of the word *ought*, he simply appeals to a skyhook called Moral Commitment.

No ideal observer. The fact that Harsanyi offers two defenses of utilitarianism is an inevitable source of confusion, but from now on attention will be paid only to his second defense, using the device of the original position that he invented

---

[5] Mathematicians will note that the von Neumann and Morgenstern utility function whose expected value must be maximized to obtain Harsanyi's utilitarian outcome is defined on the set of degenerate lotteries in which who will turn out to be whom in the original position is certain. Its values at these outcomes are just the weighted von Neumann and Morgenstern utilities of the citizens.

[6] Hare attributes his ideal observer defense of utilitarianism to Clarence Lewis. Harsanyi attributes his ideal observer defense to the same William Vickrey mentioned in the chapter on Edgeworth.

independently of Rawls at about the same time. In this second defense—previewed already in the chapter on Rawls—Harsanyi's ideal observer is replaced by actual citizens who are imagined to bargain about what is fair for their society behind a veil of ignorance that conceals what their own position in that society will be.

Equal probabilities? Critics mistakenly attach much importance to Harsanyi's assigning equal probabilities to all the different ways that people might be assigned roles in the society they agree upon in the original position.

Such critics often emphasize their concern over this issue by calling Harsanyi's theory an *equiprobability* theory of making moral judgments. Usually, they imagine that the equiprobability assumption somehow follows from Harsanyi's enthusiasm for Bayesianism.[7] But no appeal to Bayesianism is needed to justify Harsanyi's contention that Alice and Bob will assign equal subjective probabilities to the two possible outcomes possible when they emerge from behind his veil of ignorance. As in the case of Rawls, it can be taken as part of the *definition* of the original position that Alice and Bob are treated symmetrically.

Nor would it matter much to Harsanyi's argument if his equiprobable assumption were abandoned. If people behind the veil of ignorance thought it twice as likely that they would turn out to be Alice rather than Bob, all that would happen is that the weights in Harsanyi's utilitarian sum would now favor Alice over Bob, but this change in the weighting could simply be absorbed into how Alice's utility is compared with Bob's. But how is this to be explained to critics who sometimes do not even notice that Harsanyi weights the utilities of individual citizens before adding them?

What such critics need to challenge is the assumption that probabilities can be meaningfully assigned to whether someone in the original position will turn out to be Alice or Bob. But if Savage's theory of maximizing subjective expected utility[8] is to be denied in this simplest of all possible cases, then it has to be rejected altogether. Someone who wants to defend Rawls' use of the maximin criterion by denying that probabilities can meaningfully be assigned to who will turn out to be Alice or Bob, therefore needs to be aware that such an assumption would be comparable for rational decision theory with Samson bringing down the temple on the heads of the Philistines.

Empathetic preferences. In his chapter, Hare discusses why he believes it necessary to attribute empathetic preferences to an ideal observer tasked with applying

---

[7] The *objective* probability of rolling a pair of sixes with two fair dice is 1/36 because this is the frequency with which this event will occur in the long run, but one can do no such experiment when betting on whether *Punter's Folly* will win the Kentucky Derby next Saturday. Jimmy Savage extended the von Neumann and Morgenstern theory to such cases. His conclusion was that to be consistent, Alice must behave as though she were equipped with *subjective* probabilities for all events—even for events about which she is totally uninformed. Savage thought this theory of subjective expected utility only makes sense in what he called a small world, but Bayesianism is the doctrine that his theory applies in all worlds, no matter how large.

[8] Savage's theory is usually called Bayesian decision theory, but I refer to it here as a theory of subjective expected utility because critics seem unable to distinguish between Bayesian decision theory and Bayesianism.

the Golden Rule to determine what is fair in a society. His arguments apply equally well to people in the original position. They need to be equipped with empathetic preferences to be able to bargain meaningfully behind the veil of ignorance. Otherwise they would not be able to say whether they would prefer to be Alice or Bob in all of the various social contacts on which they might agree.

It is particularly important not to confuse empathetic preferences with the sympathetic preferences mentioned first in the chapter on Hume.[9] If Alice sympathizes with Bob, she will be prepared to sacrifice something of her own welfare to enhance his. If Alice merely empathizes with Bob, she may recognize that she would prefer not to be in his shoes, but her personal preferences offer no motivation for her to offer any help.

This last point establishes a link between Harsanyi and Hutcheson, Harsanyi's empathetic preferences are to be compared with Hutcheson's moral preferences. Harsanyi agrees with Hutcheson that it is necessary to make a sharp distinction between such moral preferences and our personal preferences. Charlotte's personal preferences describe whether she likes coffee better than tea. Her empathetic preferences describe whether she thinks Alice is more worthy than Bob for a social handout. According to both Harsanyi and Hutcheson, these two judgements live in totally different worlds.

15.4 Interpersonal Comparison

Harsanyi makes two assumptions about empathetic preferences. The first is that they satisfy the consistency requirements of the von Neumann and Morgenstern theory, and hence can be represented with a neoclassical utility scale. The second is that when Alice imagines herself in Bob's shoes, she is completely successful in this enterprise.[10] In particular, she recognizes that if she were Bob, she would have his preferences rather than her own. For example, Alice may prefer tea to coffee, but if she empathizes successfully with Bob, she will accept that if she were Bob, she would prefer coffee to tea if that is his preference.

Harsanyi's so-called theorems. Harsanyi is credited with two theorems: an Aggregation Theorem and an Impartial Observer Theorem, which are both essentially the same. Mathematicians think it a joke that such results should be called theorems, as though some heavy thinking was required to understand them. Harsanyi's contribution is not mathematical at all. Indeed, Harsanyi was only an amateur mathematician, whose first paper on utilitarianism contains an elementary mistake. Harsanyi's contribution is philosophical, in that he put his finger on what needs to be assumed to *trivialize* the problem of interpersonal comparison.

Harsanyi's argument goes like this. Recall his assumption that if Charlotte is in the original position, she will accept that if she were to become Alice when emerging

---

[9]It does not help that the philosopher Patrick Suppes—who deserves the credit for being the first to model empathetic preferences—called them extended sympathy preferences.

[10]This requirement seems to me the chief obstacle in applying the original position except among people who know each other very well.

from behind the veil of ignorance, she would have the same personal preferences as Alice. If she turned out to be Bob, then she will have the same personal preferences as Bob. We can therefore use Charlotte's empathetic preferences to measure by how much she would prefer to be Alice with Alice's personal preferences rather than Bob with Bob's personal preferences.

But if Charlotte's empathetic utility function describes the same preferences as Alice's personal utility function, the two von Neumann and Morgenstern utility scales that describe these preferences can differ only in their choice of zero and unit. The same goes for Bob. It follows that, from Charlotte's point of view, Alice and Bob's utility scales differ only in their choice of zero and unit. If they happen to differ in exactly the same way that degrees Celsius differ from degrees Fahrenheit, Charlotte will then be trading off Alice's personal utils against Bob's personal utils so that 5 of Alice's utils are regarded as being worth the same as 9 of Bob's utils.

Alice's utils must then be divided by 5, and Bob's utils by 9, before adding them. Or to say the same thing another way, Alice's utils need to be weighted by one fifth and Bob's utils by one ninth before they are added. So the weighted utilitarian sum of an outcome in which Alice gets 20 of her utils and Bob gets 27 of his utils is 7 (which is $\frac{1}{5} \times 20 + \frac{1}{9} \times 27$).

In brief, before applying Bentham's principle that each is to count for one, and no one to count for more than one, we need to weight Alice and Bob's personal utility scales so that they can meaningfully be treated as being equally worthy.

Social consensus on interpersonal comparison? Harsanyi did not share my naturalistic instincts at all. He was even more of a Kantian than Rawls. His argument for why everybody in the original position should be assumed to have the same empathetic preferences is a case in point.

Recall that Rawls offered the empirical observation that there seems to be a broad social consensus on how interpersonal comparisons should be made. Harsanyi agrees with this assessment, but does not find it adequate. He therefore offers the following skyhook that game theorists call the Harsanyi Doctrine when it is applied in their discipline.

15.5 Harsanyi Doctrine?

The Harsanyi Doctrine says that rationality will lead people in exactly the same situation to make the same decision. Harsanyi therefore proposes a veil of ignorance so thick that Alice and Bob recall nothing whatever of their personal lives before entering the original position. In particular, they forget their empathetic preferences, and so must construct them anew. Since their state of complete ignorance is then the same for both Alice and Bob, the Harsanyi Doctrine says that they will both construct the same empathetic preferences—that is to say, there is supposedly a unique rational way of making interpersonal comparisons that we can discover by clearing our minds of all distractions!

My own view is that such metaphysical speculation is an empty exercise. I think people find that the original position accords with their moral intuition because they recognize that it mimics the deep structure of the fairness norms they use in resolving the many coordination games of which everyday social life largely consists.

The empathetic preferences needed to use the original position are conventional in character; we unconsciously learn them over time by imitating those around us. If we were to deprive Alice and Bob of their real-life empathetic preferences, they would be as helpless in making fairness judgements as a chimpanzee asked to adjudicate an unfinished game of Chess. If we want to know when Alice and Bob will have the same empathetic preferences, we need to study the process of cultural evolution that shapes them—an activity that entails first studying what deal Alice and Bob would negotiate in the original position if they had different empathetic preferences.[11]

Equiprobability again. The Harsanyi Doctrine is also the source of the difficulties some critics have found in making sense of Harsanyi's inessential equiprobability assumption. If people in the original position are totally ignorant about everything, we can seemingly apply Laplace's dubious principle of insufficient reason, which says that equal probabilities should be assigned to events if we have no reason to think one more likely than another.

But worrying about this issue is just a distraction from what really matters about Harsanyi's contributions to utilitarian theory. It certainly has nothing to do with Harsanyi's solution of the interpersonal comparison problem as some critics seem to think.

Throwing out the Harsanyi Doctrine? It is a pity that Harsanyi's playing with a doubtful metaphysical notion like the Harsanyi Doctrine should have led to his other ideas being misunderstood by some critics. But if we throw out the Harsanyi Doctrine, it can no longer be said that Harsanyi establishes an *absolute* criterion for making interpersonal comparison. All that can be said is that his standard of interpersonal comparison is a *relative* concept depending on the social consensus in a particular society. Personally, I think this step in the direction of realism is to be welcomed.

I therefore suggest that we separate the part of Harsanyi's utilitarian theory that depends on the Harsanyi Doctrine from the part that does not depend on the Harsanyi Doctrine, which he needs only to justify the assumption that people in the original position will have the same empathetic preferences. Without the Harsanyi Doctrine, the question of why people in the original position will have the same empathetic preferences remains unanswered, but we do not need to imagine that Harsanyi solved every single problem in the foundations of utilitarianism to accord him the respect he deserves for solving the problem of interpersonal comparison.

Similar considerations apply to all the thinkers discussed in this book. We do not have to agree with everything they say to admire their efforts. Still less should we be assessing them by their mistakes. They need to be assessed by the intellectual mountains they succeeded in climbing rather than those that proved beyond their

---

[11] Pages 152–157 in my *Natural Justice*.

powers. We do not, for example, criticize Isaac Newton for failing to make any headway with either alchemy or numerology, but glory in his discovery of the law of gravitation. Why do we not treat philosophers in the same way, even when their triumphs are surpassed by later work, as Newton's model of how gravity works was surpassed by Einstein's theory of relativity?

15.6 Harsanyi's Life

I knew John Harsanyi (1920–2000) a lot better than Rawls. We often disputed his very determined attachment to Bayesianism. His in-your-face but good-natured style of disputation made him a pleasure to talk to, although I never succeeded in shaking either his Kantian convictions, or his utter devotion to Bayesianism.

As a Jew in Hungary, during the Second World War, he escaped the death camps by the skin of his teeth. He told me that he was left untouched by the first and second round-up of Jews because his role as assistant in his parent's pharmacy counted as a reserved occupation. He did not escape the third round-up, but somehow managed to 'slip away' at the railway station.

Having evaded the death camps of the Nazis, he was then forced to cross illegally into Austria with his beautiful wife to escape persecution by the Communists who followed. And once in the West, he had to build his career again from scratch, beginning with a factory job in Australia.

It was a long haul to work his way up from such humble beginnings to a Nobel prize. He was eventually lucky enough to be taken on as a graduate student at Stanford by the great economist Ken Arrow, but his unorthodox background and radical ideas meant that he was no more taken to its heart by the economics profession than he was by the philosophy profession at a later stage. In fact, he ended up as a professor in the Management School at Berkeley, publishing his great 1967 paper on incomplete information in the journal *Management Science*.

Nobel prize. In standard game theory, the types of the players—their preferences and beliefs—are assumed to be common knowledge, but what if they are not? Harsanyi's theory of incomplete information that won him the 1994 Nobel prize for economics is a way of getting a handle on this problem. It is a technique for *completing* a strategic structure in which information is incomplete.

The cleverness of Harsanyi's formulation only becomes apparent when one realizes how it avoids an infinite regress. To see how an infinite regress may arise, consider Alice and Bob after the deal in Poker. Alice doesn't know what hand Bob is holding. Bob doesn't know what Alice believes about the hand he is holding. Alice doesn't know what Bob believes about what she believes about the hand he is holding. And so on. The chain of beliefs about beliefs is closed in Poker because the chance move that represents shuffling and dealing the cards is common knowledge among the players. Harsanyi closes the chain of beliefs in the general case when information is incomplete by *inventing* a preliminary chance move that assigns types to the players. Justifying the necessary assumption that this casting move is common knowledge is sometimes problematic, but his theory allows game theorists access to a whole new range of applications. I used the theory a lot myself when designing big-money telecom auctions at the turn of the last century.

Philosophical reputation. Although I am by no means the only one to try to redress the balance, there seems little chance that John Harsanyi will eventually be recognized as one of the leading philosophers of the twentieth century.

Perhaps things would have been different if he had been able to finish the book for philosophers he was writing when he died in the year 2000. I have seen the opening chapters, but he had not got far enough to make publication of his draft feasible. The unwieldy title *Rational Behavior and Bargaining Equilibrium in Games and Social Situations* of the actual book in which Harsanyi concealed his utilitarian discoveries—beneath a mountain of unnecessary mathematics—goes a long way to explaining why he is not better appreciated. I wonder how many other innovative scholars languish in obscurity for similar reasons while the writers of tedious footnotes to Plato enjoy the plaudits of their profession?

15.7 Bentham's Unfinished Agenda

To disallow the Harsanyi Doctrine is to accept that Harsanyi failed to solve the problem of why we should expect there to be a rational consensus on how interpersonal comparisons should be made, but this problem was not raised by Bentham, nor seemingly addressed at all until he and Rawls invented the original position. As philosophers often comment, recognizing that a problem exists is a necessary first step in solving it. But what of the questions that Bentham did recognize?

How is utility measured? Harsanyi's answer is that they are to be measured in the same way that von Neumann and Morgenstern utilities are measured.

How are the utilities of different people to be compared? Harsanyi's answer is that one can deduce a rate at which we should trade Alice's utils off against Bob's utils if sufficient assumptions are made about our empathetic preferences. When a common rate exists, it determines weights that should be used to adjust Alice and Bob's utilities before they are added in a utilitarian analysis.

Why add the utilities of different people? Harsanyi's answer is covered in the chapter on Rawls. He retells Edgeworth's insurance argument in terms of the original position. If Alice and Bob are modeled as identical maximizers of expected utility behind the veil of ignorance, they will agree on a society in which average utility in society as a whole is maximized. If the size of society is fixed, maximizing average utility is the same as maximizing the sum of everybody's utility.

Why should I maximize the sum of utilities rather than my own? On this subject, Harsanyi was fixated on regarding utilitarianism as a system of personal morality rather than a recipe for determining the public policy of a benign government. He therefore invents a skyhook called Moral Commitment that is essentially the same as Rawls' Natural Duty to paper over the problem of why rationality should induce Alice to ignore her own private interest in favor of the public good. However, I do not see why we cannot simply reinterpret the work of both Harsanyi and Rawls as a way for Alice and Bob to coordinate their choice of what kind of government they wish to support in the manner recommended by Helvétius.

Further Reading

Beccaria, Cesare: *On Crimes and Punishments.* (Still relevant today.)

Bentham, Jeremy: *An Introduction to the Principles of Morals and Legislation.*

Bentham, Jeremy: *Anarchical Fallacies; Being an examination of the Declaration of Rights issued during the French Revolution.*

Binmore, Ken: *Game Theory and the Social Contract.* (In two volumes: *Playing Fair* and *Just Playing*).

Binmore, Ken: *Natural Justice.*

Binmore, Ken: *Crooked Thinking or Straight Talk?*

Binmore, Ken: *Imaginary Philosophical Dialogues.*

Broome, John: *Weighing Goods.*

Downie, Robin: *Frances Hutcheson: Philosophical Writings.*

Harsanyi, John: *Rational Behavior and Bargaining Equilibrium in Games and Social Situations.*

Hollander, Samuel: *A History of Utilitarian Ethics.*

Hume, David: *Moral Philosophy.* (A well-chosen collection of extracts from the work of David Hume compiled by Geoffrey Sayre-McCord.)

Keynes, John Maynard: *Obituary of Francis Edgeworth.* (Not a book, but can be googled.)

Mandeville, Bernard: *Fable of the Bees.*

Mill, John Stuart: *Utilitarianism.*

Mill, John Stuart: *On Liberty.*

Mill, John Stuart: *Autobiography.*

Narens, Louis and Skyrms, Brian: *The Pursuit of Happiness.*

Parfit, Derek: *Equality or Priority.* (Not a book, but the transcript of a lecture that can be googled.)

Rawls, John: *Theory of Justice.*

Rawls, John: *Political Liberalism.*

Reid, Thomas: *Common Sense*

Sen, Amartya and Bernard Williams: *Utilitarianism and Beyond*. (The authors are more interested in what lies beyond utilitarianism, but they include essays by Hare and Harsanyi.)

Schneewind, Jerome: *Sidgwick's Ethics and Victorian Moral Philosophy*.

Schofield, Philip: *Bentham: A Guide for the Perplexed*.

Smith, Adam: *Theory of Moral Sentiments*.

Smith, David Warner: *Helvétius: A Study in Persecution*.

St Clair, William: *The Godwins and the Shelleys*.

Index

act utilitarianism, 20, 65
Adams, John, 31
Aggregation Theorem, 85
Aikenhead, Thomas, 10
akrasia, 65
Aquinas, St Thomas, 4
archangels, 65
Argument by Design, 5
Aristotle, 3, 25, 80
Ashley-Cooper, Anthony, 4
Austin, John, 63
auto-icon, 43

Balfour, Arthur, 57
Bayesianism, 84, 88
Beccaria, Cesare, 7, 17, 29, 39, 56
Bentham, Jeremy, 1, 3, 7, 8, 12, 17, 25, 29, 31, 34, 39, 40, 42, 44, 47, 49, 56, 63, 66, 79
Berlin, Isaiah, 39
Bernoulli, Daniel, 24
Bernoulli, Nicolaus, 24
Bertrand-Edgeworth model, 61
Blavatsky, Madame, 58
Bolivar, Simon, 44
Boswell, James, 24
Bouffler, Countess de, 18
Broome, John, 3, 79
Burke, Edmund, 26, 35

cardinal utility, 51, 53, 81, 83
categorical imperative, 14, 34, 65
Catherine the Great, 18, 31
causal utility fallacy, 25
Chicago school, 52, 59, 63, 80
Coase, Ronald, 71
Coleridge, Samuel, 35, 48, 49
Column Duplication, 74
Column Linearity, 73
consequentialism, 14
contract curve, 71
convention, 15, 27, 76–78
Cromwell, Oliver, 6

d'Alembert, Jean, 18
Darwin, Charles, 41

deism, 12, 35
Democritus, 1, 12, 19
Dennett, Daniel, 14
deontology, 14
Dickens, Charles, 40
Diderot, Denis, 5, 17, 18
difference principle, 72
Downie, Robin, 11

Earls of Shaftesbury, 4
Edgeworth box, 61
Edgeworth series, 62
Edgeworth, Francis, 12, 43, 59, 60, 66, 69
egalitarianism, 69, 70, 77
emotivism, 63
empathetic preferences, 67
empathy, 26, 71, 78, 85
empiricism, 5, 10, 14
Encyclopédie, 9, 17, 18
enforcement, 15, 30, 56, 60, 70, 76–78
English Civil War, 4
enlightenment, 4, 19
Epicurus, 1, 3, 12, 19, 34, 41, 66
equilibrium selection device, 77
expectation, 24
expected value, 24
extended sympathy, 85

Fable of the Bees, 15
Farber, Paul, 77
felicific calculus, 59
felicity, 25, 42
Fenelon, Archbishop, 34
fitness, 14
Frankenstein, 37
Frederick the Great, 17, 21, 31

Gassendi, Pierre, 20
Gay, John, 4
Gelman, Andrew, 13
general will, 19
Gibbard, Alan, 79
Gilboa, Itzhak, 74
Glorious Revolution, 4, 10
Godwin, William, 5, 16, 30, 33, 34, 56
Golden Rule, 71, 85

© The Editor(s) (if applicable) and The Author(s), under exclusive license to Springer Nature Switzerland AG 2021
K. Binmore, *Early Utilitarians*,
https://doi.org/10.1007/978-3-030-74583-7

Good, the, 3, 55
Gossen, Hermann, 52
Graffigny, Madame de, 18
greatest happiness for the greatest number, 9, 12, 29, 39
Grotius, Hugo, 15

happiness, 1, 3, 25, 41–43, 48, 64, 80, 81
Hare, Richard, 26, 60, 63, 69, 84
Harsanyi Doctrine, 86
Harsanyi, John, 1, 14, 20, 26, 40, 42, 43, 53, 56, 63, 67, 70, 79, 88
Hazlitt, William, 35
hedonic utilitarianism, 42, 64, 80
hedonism, 25, 64
hedonism, ethical, 56, 60
hedonism, psychological, 56, 60
Heloise, 19
Helvetius, Claude, 5, 9, 14, 17, 19, 30, 35, 39, 56, 60, 65, 90
Hobbes, Thomas, 5, 15, 19, 60
Holbach, Baron d', 18, 19, 35
Hume, David, 1, 5, 9–11, 13–15, 18, 23, 24, 26, 27, 30, 31, 43, 54, 56, 64, 67, 77
Hutcheson, Francis, 1, 5, 8–10, 17, 19, 24, 26, 33, 39, 56, 69, 70, 85

ideal observer, 60, 74
Impartial Observer Theorem, 85
impartial spectator, 60
incomplete information, 88
insurance argument for utilitarianism, 59, 60, 72, 78, 81, 83, 89
interpersonal comparison, 42, 60, 75, 77, 82, 89
invisible hand, 53

Jefferson, Thomas, 31
Jevons, William, 51, 53, 54, 62, 63
Johnson, Samuel, 35

Kant, Immanuel, 11, 13–15, 34, 50, 55, 57, 63, 64, 69
Keynes, John Maynard, 56
Kropotkin, Peter, 34

Laguna, Theodore de, 77
Lamb, Charles, 35
Laplace, Pierre-Simon, 87
Leibniz, Gottfried, 33, 39
Lewis, Clarence, 66, 83
Locke, John, 4, 10, 15, 16, 26, 30
London School of Economics, 53
Louis XV, 17, 19

Machiavelli, Niccolo, 5
Madison, James, 20, 44
Mandeville, Bernard, 15

marginal utility, 25, 44, 51, 61
marginalist revolution, 52
Marshall, Alfred, 52, 57, 62
Marx, Karl, 16
maximin criterion, 70, 72–74
Mettrie, Julien de la, 18
Mill, James, 47
Mill, John Stuart, 3, 12, 23, 25, 31, 39, 47, 49, 51, 56, 57, 62, 64, 79, 80
Milnor, James, 73
Mirrlees, James, 61
Monroe, James, 36
Montaigne, Michel de, 20
Montesquieu, Charles, 17
Moore, George, 55, 57
moral commitment, 14, 19, 40, 76, 90
moral intuition, 19, 70, 77
moral law, 57
moral relativism, 66
moral sense, 5, 15
Morgenstern, Oskar, 53, 79, 81
moths, 39, 43, 48, 55

Narens, Louis, 25
Nash equilibrium, 15, 77
natural duty, 14, 19, 40, 70, 76
natural law, 10, 26, 40
natural right, 16, 40
naturalism, 9, 12, 26, 57
naturalistic fallacy, 55
neoclassical economics, 25, 42, 51, 53, 80, 81
neoclassical utility, 80
neoplatonism, 4
Newton, Isaac, 40, 54, 88
noble savage, 16

ordinal utility, 52
original position, 69–71, 74
Owen, Robert, 16, 36

Paine, Tom, 35, 36
Panopticon, 43
Pareto efficiency, 52, 61, 71, 73
Pareto, Vilfredo, 52
Parfit, Derek, 12, 72, 73, 75
perfectly competition, 53
philosophes, les, 17
Plato, 3
Plotinus, 4
point of view of the universe, 60
preference utilitarian, 80
preference utilitarianism, 64
preference utilitarians, 42
primary goods, 74
prioritarianism, 72
proles, 65
Pufendorf, Samuel von, 15

Index

rationalism, 3, 14, 34, 57
Rawls' principles of justice, 72
Rawls, John, 1, 14, 20, 40, 55, 69, 72, 76, 79
reason, pure and practical, 56
reciprocity, 27
reflective equilibrium, 70
Reid, Thomas, 10, 11
relativism, moral, 15, 28
repugnant conclusion, 12, 75
revealed preference, 25, 42, 81
Ricardo, David, 45, 53
Robbins, Lionel, 53, 81, 82
Robespierre, Maximilien, 31, 36
romanticism, 16, 19
Rousseau, Jean-Jacques, 15, 16, 18
Rudin's axiom, 73
rule utilitarianism, 20, 65
Russell, Bertrand, 57

Samuelson, Paul, 81
Savage, Jimmy, 25, 84
Sayre-McCord, Geoffrey, 24
Schmeidler, David, 74
Scottish enlightenment, 9
Sen, Amartya, 80, 83
Shaftesbury, Lord, 4, 9, 30
Shelley, Percy Bysse, 36, 37
Sheridan, Richard, 35
Sidgwick, Henry, 31, 55, 57, 60, 62, 65, 70
Singer, Peter, 60, 63
skyhook, 14, 39, 43, 48, 54, 55, 60, 65, 76, 86, 90
Skyrms, Brian, 25
Smith, Adam, 10, 11, 24, 26, 43, 45, 53, 60, 67
social contract, 5, 15, 19, 72
Spencer, Herbert, 54
St Francis of Assisi, 13, 80
St Petersburg paradox, 24
state of nature, 5, 15, 16
Stoicism, 4
strains of commitment, 70
summum bonum, 57
Suppes, Patrick, 85
sympathetic preferences, 13
sympathy, 26, 80, 85

taxation, 60
Taylor, Harriet, 48
termites, 39, 43, 48, 55, 70

universalizability, 66
University College London, 45, 53
utilitarian, 43, 69
utilitarianism, definition, 12
utility, 9, 24, 42, 81
utopianism, 33, 36

veil of ignorance, 60, 71, 74, 85

Vickrey, William, 59, 61, 83
Vienna Circle, 63
Voltaire, 5, 18, 33
von Neumann and Morgenstern utility, 53, 79
von Neumann, John, 53, 79

Wedgewood, Josiah, 16, 36
Wedgewood, Thomas, 36
Will, the, 57, 65
Williams, Bernard, 77
Wollstencraft, Mary, 34, 36, 37, 48

Zayid, 20
Zeno, of Citium, 4

GPSR Compliance

The European Union's (EU) General Product Safety Regulation (GPSR) is a set of rules that requires consumer products to be safe and our obligations to ensure this.

If you have any concerns about our products, you can contact us on

ProductSafety@springernature.com

In case Publisher is established outside the EU, the EU authorized representative is:

Springer Nature Customer Service Center GmbH
Europaplatz 3
69115 Heidelberg, Germany

www.ingramcontent.com/pod-product-compliance
Lightning Source LLC
LaVergne TN
LVHW010344260326
834688LV00036B/873